Ireland:
Beyond the Pale

ireland:
BEYOND THE PALE

J.A. PATRINA

JOE PATRINA is a singer/songwriter based in West Simsbury, Connecticut, where he leads the popular country/rock group LittleHouse. As with his songwriting, Joe applies his seasoned observational skills and to-the-point writing style to pen insightful works on sports, history, politics, medicine, and music, seamlessly interweaving these disparate elements to create a unique brand of travelogues in place and time.

A cofounder of Wall Street Systems, Joe brings his lifetime of experience at a global level to his musical and literary endeavors.

Copyright © 2019 by J.A. Patrina.

All rights reserved. No part of this book may be reproduced in any form or by any electronic or mechanical means, including information storage and retrieval systems, without permission in writing from the publisher, except by reviewers, who may quote brief passages in a review.

ISBN: 978-1-7330672-9-4   [Paperback Edition]

Printed and bound in The United States of America.
 Published by LittleHouse Enterprises Inc.

Prelude

Why in God's name did you come here? The redheaded Irish woman in the pub asks after I announce our family's Irish tour.

Do you have some Irish in you? She continues.

Plenty, I respond with a laugh, *and my wife, too, but that's not why we're here.*

Why on earth then?

The weather.

The weather? This isn't weather, dear; this is rain!

She would neither prove the last nor the first incredulous Irish person to contemplate the wisdom of dragging an American wife and four teenaged children to Ireland.

After all, the calendar read "August," with the entire world our oyster offering other destinations from which to choose, and we – I – chose Ireland.

The implication: The Irish, the sad Irish history and Ireland's disappointing weather strongly suggested alternate plans.

But Irish melancholies make a long story, and before I attempt to explain them, let's get back to the rain.

In Ireland, the typical August forecast projects partly cloudy skies with temperatures in the upper 60s.

In Connecticut, where I live, this makes for a perfect day... on Halloween!

But after a few days of cross footing the *forecast* against *actual* Irish weather, I soon learn that in Ireland, *partly cloudy* means that at some point the sun will peek through... and until then, and after then, the sky will deliver sudden bursts of drenching rain.

Some days prove better than others, but no place on Earth offers up worse weather, except perhaps *Tierra del Fuego*.

The Atlantic Ocean and its grueling weather systems, including weakening hurricanes, plow into Ireland at all hours of the day and night. Luckily, the Gulf Stream hits Ireland too; square on, keeping temperatures mild. And so, for someplace this far north, snow appears about as frequently in Dublin as it does in Dallas.

It is just as I wrote in my Irish ditty:

Everything's green in Ireland

The sun shines 'til the clouds move in

And when it rains it all begins

Hey, hey I want to stay in old Ireland

Hey, hey I want to stay in old Ireland

DAY 1
Tuesday, August 14th

We touch down at Dublin Airport.

After fetching our nine bags, my family and I climb aboard a Hertz transporter to pick up our red Volkswagen microbus, driven directly from 1972 to its space in the tiny parking lot.

I take the wheel, the only driver; no one else volunteers, probably because, as in England, Ireland's motorists *"drive on the wrong side of the road."*

There. I've said it. But every driver on the planet must share the world's view of where a vehicle belongs relative to the centerline!

In years past, my wife Laura logged miles on both English and Irish roads, but, as she points out, that was *before we had children*. By this, I'm not sure if she means that in caring for our children's safety she prefers that today I do all the driving, or … if she simply prefers to now enjoy the landscape.

Either way, our tally shows that Laura and my two driving age daughters pass on sharing the driving, and I am to serve as the sole chauffeur.

And so it comes to be... It's all me, all the time, behind the wheel on the wrong side of the rode.

Traveling north on the highway we seek Castle Leslie, our first destination, located in Monaghan County, on the border with Northern Ireland, and my wife begins yelling at me for driving too slowly... *everyone is passing us!*

I momentarily lose my temper, and then explain... *Let them pass. I'm trying to get my sea legs for driving on the left. There are all kinds of ways for me to mess up ... all right?*

Silence.

My 19-year-old daughter slaps the map out of my wife's hands, thus usurping her position of navigator, and, within minutes, the new navigator begins yelling at me.

Dad, you need to start passing the trucks.

Things settle down. Then I see it, a highway sign that marks the *River Boyne*, in Gaelic and English.

This river valley is, to me, the center of Ireland. Recently in 1690, the Irish fought a losing battle alongside James Stuart II, England's short term Catholic King, fighting against William of Orange, the incoming English Protestant King imported from Holland. This collision transpired up valley in the *"Battle of the Boyne"*.

Before that, a thousand years further back, the Boyne hosted the meeting place of the Irish Kings at a place called *Tara*. They discussed life and death.

And further back, around 4,000 years ago, ancient Pre-Celtic peoples dwelled at a place called *Newgrange*. There "The Architect" built a round house, so that on the December 21st equinox, a ray of morning sunlight could pierce a stone shaft and illuminate a carved stone bowl hidden deep in the middle of the round structure - all for the purpose of paying respect to Irish ancestors.

Seeing the River Boyne ignites my romanticism, and I can finally drive through the jet lag.

After a while, we arrive at Castle Leslie, an equestrian-focused destination, with 1,000 acres of land, an ample stable of horses, and a baronet titled "Sir John Leslie."

We stay in the hunting lodge rather than the manor house, but we find it perfect.

My family of six enjoys three rooms in a separate section of the lodge, and, best of all, the lodge includes the restaurant, the spa, the stables... and, most importantly, the pub.

The Castle Leslie Estate anchors the village of *Glaslough* in Monaghan County, and the Castle pub <u>is</u> the village pub, so action abounds at all times of the day and night.

Checking in, during a break in the rain, we enjoy an early pub dinner and hang out there for the evening: tomorrow, the horses!

Above: The Horses

Below: Newgrange and The River Boyne

Below: Traditional Houses

Our host: Sir John Leslie

DAY 2
Wednesday, August 15th

The next morning the rain stays away, and after breakfast the whole family strolls over to the manor house. The thermometer reads an even 60 degrees Fahrenheit, and a mid-August fire burns in the Castle Leslie hearth behind an empty reception desk.

No one occupies the dining room either. We enter the living room, also empty of humans but filled with Leslie family memorabilia, antiques, carpets, and large windows overlooking the mile-long lake and surrounding grounds.

The room boasts an old grand piano made in Berlin, kept in perfect tune.

I play piano, as do two of my three daughters.

Jolene, why don't you play one of your pieces? I urge my youngest daughter.

She gives it a go but stumbles a little, saying that the piano sounds different from the one we have at home. I reassure her: *Yes, it sounds a bit brighter, but it is a fabulous piano. Go ahead and play something.*

She plays an intricate piece, and then Codyann, my eldest plays a few classical pieces as well. The music rings through the mansion, but still, not a living soul in sight. We step through the side French doors onto the patio leading to acres of mowed lawns that reach down to the lake.

My son Joe and I put on our baseball mitts and begin our "long toss" exercise program as the girls wander off to the boathouse. Joe counts baseball as his main sport, so we throw most days on these trips to keep his arm in shape.

Often, as we throw across a good 120-foot distance, Europeans, who have never seen an American hardball, stop us to hold the ball, realizing only then the underlying danger of the sport.

At about 11:00 AM, we remember that our first two-hour equestrian outing starts soon at 12:15 PM; we have to get going. To return to the Hunting Lodge, we cut back through the mansion, as fences or walls block all other exits of the inner mansion grounds.

Inside the living room I decide not to simply march on through, as it dawns on me that my turn to play the German piano has come up in rotation. My family politely sits and I sing *Sweet Noreen*, one of my favorite compositions - about a father and daughter whose relationship has unraveled. Realizing that I had only just started, the family impatiently hurries back out to explore again.

Alone, I play another composition of mine called *Ireland*.

She was a green- eyed lady from Ireland
Red hair and curls and silken skin
Oh I'd like to love her all over again

Well this ship's going to Ireland
When the tide comes in they'll sail her down the river
And I've made up my mind I'm going with her

Well shiver me timbers and anchors away
Haul in that line we'll sail her away
Wind's at our back and the sun be shining today
Salt's in the air and the wind be blowin' my way

Well I walked out the door I just walked away
A man's got to know when to go when to stay
But I'd love to love her all over one day.

As I finish the song, I look up. An old man, perhaps in the second half of his nineties, stands in the doorway, thin and trim, dressed in a tweed blazer, wearing a woolen necktie. He speaks.

That piano belonged to Lady Randolph Churchill, Winston's mother.

I knew at once that he was Leslie, who, as a British officer had been a prisoner-of-war from 1940 until 1945.

The Germans captured his rear guard unit (an Irish Guard unit), but not until a few hundred thousand British and Allied troupes successfully evacuated the beaches of Dunkirk shortly after Hitler's blitzkrieg caught the world by surprise at the outset of the war.

I pretend not to know who he is. I stand up, walk over and extend my hand, saying:

Then I am most fortunate, as my four heroes in history have boiled down to Franklin, Washington, Lincoln and Churchill. My name is Joe Patrina; I am staying here with my family for four nights.

He shakes my hand and responds: *I'm John Leslie and I live here.*

Suddenly out of nowhere a voice chimes in, solemnly pronouncing:

That's SIR John Leslie.

It is Sir John's butler making certain I know to whom I speak. I express my pleasure in meeting both of them, adding that I hoped my piano playing had not disturbed the house.

Sir John replies that he does not hear in one ear, due to a war injury, and so my playing, good or bad, does not affect him, but it delights him that I affirm the Churchill piano to still hold its tuning. Sir John and his butler bid me farewell and disappear into the dinning room for a late breakfast.

I hurry back outside to find my family.

Guess whom I just met?

Yes, they agree, how wonderful that I met Sir John, but we need to get ready for our pending riding appointment at the stables.

And so, we traipse back through the Manner House for the third time, determined to return to the Hunting Lodge and change into our boots and breeches.

I nonetheless peek into the dining room. At their table, beside Sir John and his Butler, a woman has joined them. I cannot help myself, and tell the family to carry on without me as I step into the dining room. The woman looks up and says:

So you've been serenading the house this morning. I'm Samantha, Sir Leslie's niece.

Similar to other fortunate families back in the late 1500s, the Tudor Queen -- Elizabeth the 1st (below) – granted the Leslies 24,000 acres of Irish land as part of her "Plantings" program.

For centuries, ever since the original Norman Conquest spilled from England into Ireland, Ireland gradually slipped back into the hands of local Irish Chieftains. To counter this, Elizabeth (below) came up with a scheme to bring hundreds of noble English families into Ireland and "plant" them as overlords throughout the countryside.

Just to be tidy about dates, please consider, that long before Elizabeth in the 1500s, the Normans had moved into Ireland by the 1100s, soon after William of Normandy "The Conqueror" took over England in 1066. But the Irish, clever little devils; clawed most of Ireland back from the Norman/English by 1450, establishing a set of Irish Earldoms.

By 1450, The English king controlled only the area surrounding Dublin. A fortified barrier called *The Pale* delineated this last English foothold.

Inside The Pale: England.

Beyond The Pale: The Irish.

"Beyond The Pale" (this book's title) came to mean the world of wild Irish heathens, tribal beasts who knew nothing of civilized decency.

The Castle Leslie brochure boasts that the Leslie estate has remained in Leslie hands ever since Elizabeth 1st bestowed it upon them as part of *The Plantings*.

Mind you, she never gave it to them as she retained *allodial* title to the property (ownership granted from God as part of the divine right of kings), but the Leslies – so long as they stayed in the monarch's good graces - could operate the land as if it were their own, directing its operation, meting out discipline to the peasants, and collecting rents from the people who lived on the 24,000 acres.

By the way, once a king or queen granted you a sweetheart deal such as this, you obtained a status termed "Landed," hence the term "Landed Gentry."

Today the Leslies have but 1,000 acres, and I will explain what happened to the other 23,000 acres a bit later.

But let's get back to the rain.

I enter into a conversation with niece Samantha, with Sir John occasionally adding a word or two, when Codyann, my eldest, enters the dining room and asks Samantha: *Is he bothering you?*

Certainly not. We have been discussing music and where it comes from. Were you one of the pianists this morning?

I hope it was all right, Cody answers. *But I need to get dad down to the stables and he still needs to change.*

We say our goodbyes, and Cody and I leave the Castle as the rain starts to fall.

Later on, niece Samantha "Sammy" and I would converse again, she saying that the property once inspired Wordsworth, a frequent guest of the castle.

And though there is a zero-tolerance policy on naming A-list visitors, yet given my own credentials as a singer/songwriter, Sammy lets on that notable guests have included Mick Jagger, W. B. Yeats, the Prince of Monaco and Mr. Churchill himself, (whose white baby frock sits in the drawing room in a dainty frame, not to mention his mother's piano). And let's not forget that Paul (McCartney), the Beatle married here.

Back in our rooms, while dressing, the rain falls harder and harder. The family assembles, stoically marching down to the stable area to find our guide, a veteran, redheaded horse connoisseur. I asked her if she still plans to ride.

Of course, she exclaims, *you paid for it, lad, and it'll be raining during your entire stay.*

I guess you're used to going out in these conditions I comment.

No, I'm not used to it. But we all need to carry on, don't we now?

My take: this woman could make a man out of anyone.

So out we go. Two hours in a downpour and I do not notice the rain one bit. We become part of the environment, just like the horses. We'd walk, trot, and canter all over the thousand acres, arriving back as beaten up as I've ever felt. But the rain doesn't mean a thing. I guess "me Irish" was kicking in, and the same went for the whole family. We suffer from sore muscles, struggling to walk or move; but to us, the rain did not exist.

Back in our rooms, we peel off our riding garb, shower, dress, and head for the pub.

Strolling over to reception I meet up with niece Samantha again, and comment on a book for sale by her uncle, Sir John himself, titled: *Never A Dull Moment*.

Oh, we have been writing books forever, she comments.

Samantha shows me a quote from Jonathan Swift, a friend of an earlier generation of Leslies, who once wrote of the family:

Here I am in Castle Leslie,

With rows and rows of books upon the shelves,

Written by the Leslies,

All about themselves.

Ms. Leslie notes that in the 200-plus years since Mr. Swift wrote the poem—she called it a "rude ditty"—her relatives have published more than 200 books.

Apparently a biography of niece Leslie's late father, Desmond, came out around Christmas. He may have been the most eccentric member of the clan to date. A successful record producer and screenwriter who turned the family estate into a hippie commune in the 1960s, he is probably best known for his own book, entitled "Flying Saucers Have Landed," which Ms. Leslie said has been translated into 20 languages (*Desmond above*).

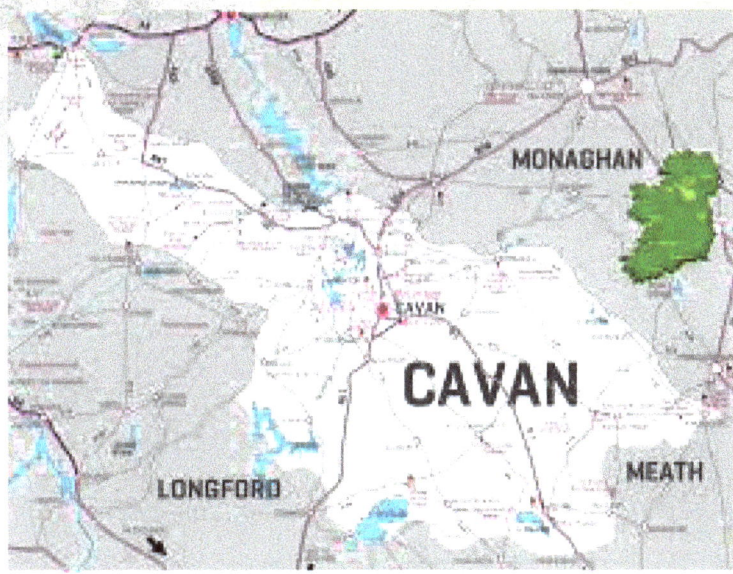

During the book conversation "Sammy" tells me to catch *Altan* (a band), tomorrow night over in Cavan (the next county over). I didn't need to be told twice.

DAY 3
Thursday, August 16th

And so, the next day, after a second AM riding excursion, we set our sights on an ambitious evening: the Celtic Music Festival taking place in Cavan, just west of Monaghan.

The Cavan Festival, a big deal, goes for eight straight days and nights, with hundreds of the best traditional artists from Ireland and elsewhere performing, some on the big stage in the tent, and the others in smaller venues and in pubs.

Just in case I might indulge in a drink or two along the way, I hire a local driver from Glaslough village for Euro 150 to be our chauffeur for the evening and night. With great expectations on my part, and the children doubtful, we ride off to the realm of music.

As a composer, I believe that one needs to let the composition and lyrics present themselves. Then you more or less assemble the final structure. Niece Samantha and I discussed this until my daughter interceded. But if you can't recognize the form of the music coming at you, then you can't assemble it.

For example, I had written a few Irish folk songs, for I knew their form, as in ...

Here we are in Ireland, driving the Dingle road
Give me love and bring me life in the times that we shall know

But I did not understand the hard-core stuff, the intense, fiddle-led compositions supported by orchestral underpinnings of guitar, mandolin, accordion, and flute, where the dual and dueling fiddles battled with evolving rapid-fire melody lines.

I wanted to write something like this for dual electric lead guitars played on Fender Stratocasters (something along the lines of *Freebird*, but more Celtic), and I hungered to hear what the best high-performance Celtic band in the world sounded, looked, and felt like.

The best band of the festival, *Altan*, according to Samantha, hailed from Donegal (Dun Na Agal).

Another excellent and popular band performing just before Altan, presented smooth, exotic blends of Celtic and Moody Blues-styled influences. But my appetite called for the Jimi Hendrix version of Celtic music, where sheer virtuosity reigned.

Outside, the rain pours. A one-acre tent covers the main stage, replete with a top-shelf sound system. I grow psyched as the stage crew prepares for Altan, and I manage to find an empty second-row seat, leaving my entire family back in Row 35 as they refuse to forage for better seats.

Sitting in my newly acquired second-row seat, I notice a gaping stage-right door, with a van idling outside. The van doors open and out steps the band *Altan*, skipping through the pounding rain into the tent area.

A gorgeous blond woman leads the charge, followed by a gallant Irishman. They prove the lead fiddle players and vocalists. Altan had driven two hours from Donegal to Cavan town, and the group, judging by their demeanor, arrives clearly keen to perform.

Despite my appreciation of the performance, as the father of four, I realize that my children, back in the 35th row, endure rather than enjoy the Celtic music. More so, they listen with empty stomachs.

I need a plan.

Right before the band comes on, I walk to the far side of the tent and look through the glass door in search of my van and driver. I see the van, but not the driver.

He ran off 10 minutes ago with his umbrella, the middle-aged, on-the-ball security woman monitoring that door informs me.

I tell her about the squeeze I face with Altan coming on and my kids starving.

I'll keep me eyes open for you, she says. *Just look over and I'll give you a nod.*

Waving to my family, implying: *Don't worry 'bout nothing*, I rush back to my second-row seat that a longhaired, redheaded, former hippie Celtic character from Derry saved for me.

I know that some of you big-city Americans from Boston, New York and Chicago think you "know the Irish" – and you do - but seeing, firsthand, these *Emerald Islanders* emerge from their countryside, seeing the *real* Irish... well...

Ok, bring out the band for heaven's sake.

Altan kills!

Everything they do kills: voices, look, animation, countenances, song pace, and the aforementioned virtuosity.

They finish an intricate fiddle piece that blows the audience away... and then erupt into an even more intense, faster-tempo piece that mesmerizes all.

They chat with the audience, providing relief, right before launching into yet another extravaganza.

At one point I swear I hear a cello quartet moving underneath the dual fiddlers. Where on Earth does it come from? I look at the accordion player, but he plays accents, not the grand, sweeping movements I hear.

Finally, I find it. The acoustic guitarist plays moving triad chord structures on the bottom three strings of his guitar, moving fluidly between the high and low frets. Masterful.

After a while I look back at the security woman. She gives me the nod. My driver has returned, hopefully sober. In the middle of another dual-fiddle piece I leave my seat and

brave the pouring rain to see the driver.

I instruct him to be ready to leave, as the rain looms far too heavy for us to prowl about the pubs in Cavan. Instead I want to go to *The Old Post House Restaurant*, which we passed driving into Cavan from Monaghan.

That's a good one, he adds, *but a bit pricy.*

On my way back to the show I face the rain pouring outside and the band pouring it on inside. Due to the tent, the rain and the distance, I now hear the music as one entity, as a symphony orchestra performing Mozart, and yet the band comprises but six pieces.

A bit later, inside the van, I find myself in a lot of family trouble over the food situation.

What makes you think the Old Post Restaurant is still open?

It just has to be.

We pull up and through the old inn's windows I can see diners still seated. So I hop out ahead of the family and jump inside to find the hostess.

Sorry, but the kitchen closed a half-hour ago.

Right then I notice a shelf of vintage Armagnac's with bottles from the 1940s onward. My eyes light up. *I knew this place was quality.*

I tell the hostess about the festival, Altan, my starving children, and my love for Armagnac ... and then I plead with her: *Can we order just an entre?*

Well, the chef's pretty temperamental, but I'll ask.

A few moments pass and she returns.

I told him you was just out seeing Altan over at the festival and he said he'll do it.

We all had big-time steaks, sides, and wine, and then sent our sincere thanks and compliments back to the chef. Finally, considering the fact that we, well, I, had a driver out there, I ordered a flight of 1970s Armagnac's to finish it off.

The Lynches - owners of The Old Post House.

Niece Samantha Leslie of Leslie Castle

DAY 4
Friday, August 17th

The next day we find ourselves back on horses for the third time, with my second daughter, Tara - named for the meeting place of the Irish Kings - riding behind me.

A bit of communication ensues... Tara begins.

You're pulling up too much. Horses only know about pulling back. Keep your hands low.

I am.

No you're not. And another thing you are leaning on the horse's neck when you canter. If the horse trips or lowers his head you're dead.

Ok.

Lean forward over the neck, hands half way up the neck with short reigns, but sink into your heels for balance. Don't rely on the neck.

All right, already!

I realize she endeavors to position me into a jockey's form. When I finally comply, everything falls into place.

Later, at the far end of the property, the guide turns to me, points to a long, wide area of marshland, and says: *That's the border.*

Of the estate? I try to clarify.

No, of the country. That hill yonder is Northern Ireland. That's the U.K.

This fact stuns me. I knew it lay near, but there it stood: the border. I am no IRA persona at all, but for sure, it felt bizarre to experience The United Kingdom on Irish soil.

In the afternoon, we fire shotguns at clay pigeons in front of the castle. Our host, a local sportsman, informs me that Ireland runs so anti-gun that it counts only 1,400 gun club members on the entire island.

I tell him that my smallish hometown of 7,000 households probably matches that total, and that ever since Obama took over, all kinds of people tell me they purchased firearms.

He expresses amazement of the American instinct to arm itself against its own government, held true ever since the ratification of 2nd amendment during America's infancy.

As it happens, that evening, after the horse and gun business ended and we returned to the pub, I notice two animated couples. One guy wears a collared shirt with the following language stitched into his sleeve: *Not Equal, Better.*

I venture over and proffer the slogan as I introduce myself to the party, a lively bunch down from Belfast in Northern Ireland for a long weekend, definitely not socialists.

We talk about America a bit and they appear disturbed by the news that during the Obama administration, the percentage of Americans paying no federal income tax grew from 40 percent to 50 percent of the households.

Then we talk about the border.

Apparently, after the 1919 Irish/English revolution, before Northern and Southern Ireland divided, Ulster, the northern region, comprised nine counties. But only six of the nine stayed with England to become today's Northern Ireland, and the three border counties – Monaghan, Cavan and Donegal – went with the south, where they remain today.

I asked how this 6-3 split of Ulster happened. My Belfast friends did not know.

They guessed that it probably resulted from a higher mix of Catholics versus Protestants in those three more southern counties.

The northern Protestants had Celtic blood, but for the most part they had emigrated back and forth from Northern Ireland to Scotland many centuries ago. The Scots later identified themselves as Presbyterians, a Protestantism branch of Christianity, and so their northern Irish kin appear different from the pure Irish Catholics in heritage and religion ... but not in blood.

They all stand as Celtics.

Shouldn't Celtic blood come first, and religious nuances second?

After all, the English proved just as brutal to the Scotts. During the Scottish Clearings after 1745, half of Scotland was either killed or sent to America and Australia.

Castle Leslie, Ireland

Why in the 1920s, when Ireland began to obtain its independence from England, did the Irish divide themselves over Catholic/Protestantism lines?

Michael Collins, the George Washington figure of Irish independence, kept asking that very question in the midst of the bickering in 1922.

Michael Collins appears as quite a figure in human history, assassinated at the age of but 31 that same year.

One mystical fact about his background notes that his father, the seventh son of a seventh son, when on his deathbed told the family to look after young Michael, then 6, as he would free Ireland.

Michael grew up brilliant, practical, intense, an eloquent dynamo, mentored by many while working in brokerage and banking houses in London.

In his private life he claimed membership in organizations bent on liberating Ireland and he became a member of the Sinn Fein political party: Sinn Fein – meaning "Ourselves Alone".

In 1919, when the big revolutionary fighting broke out, Michael served as the living brain of the revolution, running the finance/provisioning and intelligence/targeting aspects of the operation, leaving IRA captains to execute perpetual guerilla tactics throughout the country. They ran the British ragged, until Britain offered to negotiate emancipation.

Eamon de Valera, the Irish "shadow" president, selected Michael and other revolutionary luminaries to accompany Arthur Griffith – the founder of Sinn Fein - to represent Ireland in the negotiations. Churchill, working for Prime Minister Lloyd George, represented England. Collins and Griffith came home with a treaty. *(Collins, left - de Valera, right)*

The problem? The treaty made Ireland a Dominion – like Canada and Australia - it permitted protestant counties in the north to stay with the United Kingdom, and it required everyone to commit to the following oath:

I... do solemnly swear true faith and allegiance to the Constitution of the Irish Free State as by law established, and that I will be faithful to His Majesty King George V, his heirs and successors....

Collins, the practical realist, concluded that the Treaty offered Ireland "the freedom to achieve freedom." Still, upon signing the treaty, Collins remarked: *I have signed my own death warrant.*

The hard core IRA guys hated it. They were, after all, 100 percent "Ourselves Alone" warriors.

His "Free to become free" plan was meant to get the British to leave, giving the northern Protestants time to realize and accept the southern Irish as their kin.

But de Valera turned hard-core, rejecting the treaty, demanding absolute sovereignty, and siding with the IRA. The Irish, in the spring of 1922, divided, and sank into a violent civil war.

Then, in August of 1922, Michael Collin's mentor Arthur Griffith died from heart failure. Ten days later on August 22nd, the IRA shot Michael Collins dead at age 31. Sinn Fein, after all, did now truly mean "Ourselves Alone".

The Civil War, which followed – between those wanting the Collins plan and the IRA extremists -, may have claimed more lives than the War of Independence against Britain that preceded it, and it left Irish society divided.

Today, two of the main political parties in the Republic of Ireland, Fianna Fáil (a left-leaning, no-British-allowed party dominating Ireland along with de Valera ever since its formation) and Fine Gael (the party that favored the treaty and lists its core values as equality of opportunity, fiscal rectitude, free enterprise and reward, individual rights and responsibilities) prove direct descendants of the opposing sides in the war.

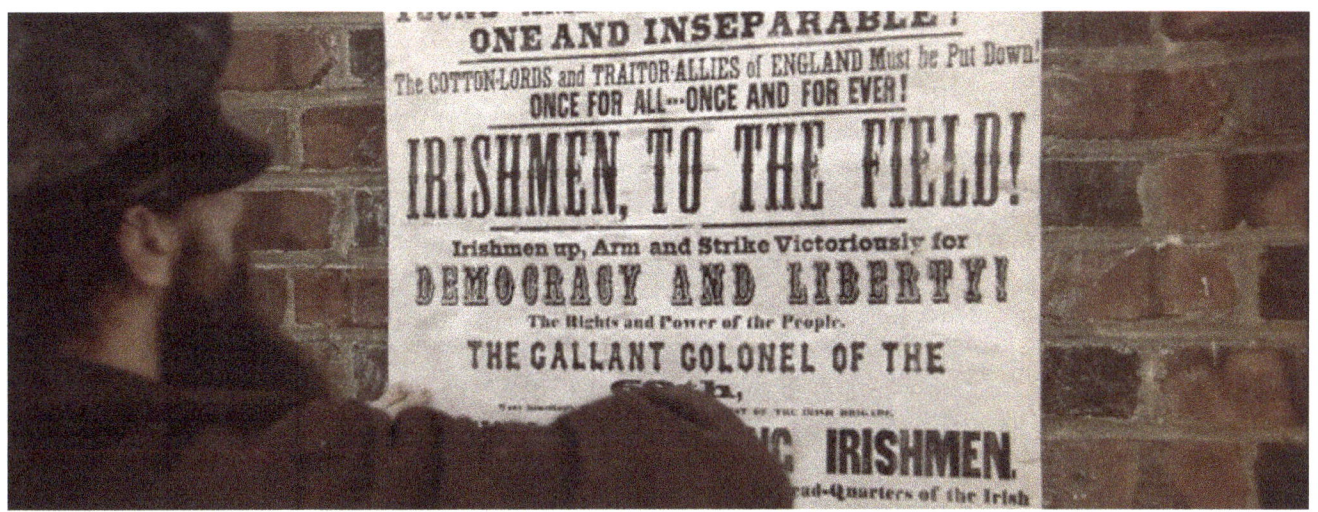

Perhaps Collins, had he lived, would have contained this, just as some believe that the USA's post-Civil War reconstruction would have proven different had Lincoln lived.

In all of this chaos, someone drew up the north/south boundary, which remains a centerpiece of the Irish psyche to this day.

DAY 5
Saturday, August 18th

Leaving Castle Leslie and Monaghan Country, we drive north to find the A3, the main east/west boundary road that will take us to our next stop, County Sligo.

At one point, the sight of a British Union Jack flying in the front yard of a homeowner gives me a distinct start.

Then I see others...

As we move westward, we cross the border numerous times, sometime seeing the green/orange Irish flags, and other times their British counterparts.

By the way, the Irish flag symbolizes the unity of the Irish – green represents the Catholics, and orange the Protestants (as in William of Orange).

Our current direction, to the west of Ireland, makes for the mountainous side of the island, and the Gaelic-speaking side, as well. The west and the Gaelic go together for the simple fact that each time the English tried from the 1100s through the 1900s to colonize Ireland, the holdout Celts managed to disappear into the desolate west to avoid subjugation.

But who are these Celtic peoples?

After the Ice Age receded, stone-age people settled the Iberian Peninsula, up the French coast and into the British Isles. In

common they built stone circles and stone burial Cairns. The Paleolithic stone ruins in Carnac France are the same as those in Scotland and Ireland.

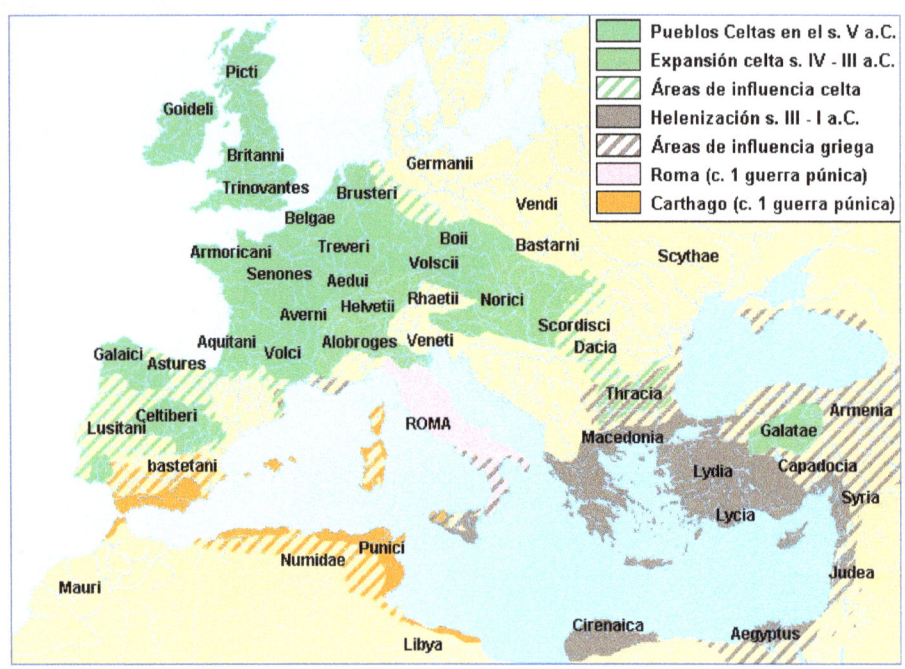

Around 600 BC, the Celts, a new race, arrive on the scene leaving their place north and east of the Alps, and settling the same lands as their stone-age predecessors had out to Ireland. The fate of the stone-age predecessors is unknown. Perhaps some intermarriage took place, but extermination is likely.

Afterwards, through marriage to non-Celtics, Celtics changed their genetic makeup. The Spanish Celtics interbred with Roman Latin's, Moors, and Jews, though today, one can still see dark red hair traits in some Spaniards. The French Gallic Celts mixed with the Roman Latin's, but they also mixed with Germanic and Norwegian bloodlines. Still many French bear the dark red hair of their original Celtic ancestors.

Ireland and Scotland, however, possess only traces of Latin and Germanic blood, as the Romans and Anglo/Saxons never made it across the Irish Sea, or above Hadrian's Wall in Scotland.

Instead Irish blood mixed with Norwegian, as the Vikings came to stay from the 800s onward.

Interestingly, Norwegians also carry the red hair gene, but a lighter and curlier red hair then the dark straight black/red hair of the pure Celt. This Celtic/Norwegian mix defined the Irish up until 1100 when the Norman English arrived.

But the Normans, also of Viking descent originally hailing from Norway, settled northwest France in the 800's. Before invading England in 1066, these French Normans intermarried with the French, also part Celtic.

So, when French-Norman (now English) barons began to dwell in Ireland after 1100, it served only to add a bit more Norwegian genetic stuff into the Irish gene pool.

I learned this the hard way, upon discovering that my own Irish heritage actually proves Norman.

By way of a blood test at age 45, I learned that my blood carried 12 times as much iron as normal. Clogging my liver, if not corrected, the imbalance would kill me by causing liver failure, the same fate suffered by my "Irish" grandfather.

For one to inherit this genetic iron-collecting trait, both parents need be carriers of a certain recessive "iron" gene passed by <u>both</u> parents to you at conception.

This "iron" gene supposedly came from Norwegian stock. But I am not Norwegian.

Or so I thought.

My maternal grandfather who possessed curly red hair in his youth, and died from liver failure, bore the name "Burke."

In 1450, the Burkes possessed an Irish earldom in the Galloway area. Upon further research, I learn that the Burkes descended from Herbert De Burghs, a Norman-English family from King John's court. The De Burghs claimed they descended directly from Charlemagne.

Considering that the De Burgh's (Burkes) lived in Ireland ever since King John set them up in the early 1200s, makes me wonder why my Burke ancestors came to America poor, providing me with no inheritance whatsoever.

The De Burges – aka The Burkes

On my father's side, the Marshalls comprise an Irish family from Cork. Henry II gave William Marshall, a Norman – who was the greatest knight of the realm - the land around Cork in the late 1100's (William right).

William sired five sons, but records indicate that they in turn had no sons, so the mystery remains as to how our Marshall name came down through history. My mother says the Marshall boys had other woman by whom males were conceived... what does she know?

One thing's for sure: The Marshalls in my day had light, strawberry-blond, curly Norwegian hair, as does my brother Jim. Still, even on the Marshall side of the equation, no inheritance, nothing!

It would seem that my Norman kin on both sides passed along nothing more than those iron-collecting genes. Thanks, folks!

Anyway, inheritance blues aside, this blend of original Celtic blood mixed in with various Norwegian/Norman bloodlines makes up the modern-day Irish person.

But as relatively pure Celtic as the Irish remain; I consider it a miracle that the Gaelic language survives at all.

At one point the English made speaking Gaelic illegal, shooting anyone fostering it.

A woman at the Leslie Castle pub told me that in the 1800s, the Irish conducted what they called "hedge schools," where the children would literally gather outside by a hedge to learn the three R's, with the reading and writing parts passed along in Gaelic.

Throughout the 1800s the English cracked down further on Celtic culture, finally disallowing the hedge schools and forcing the children into government schools.

Yikes! This sounds very much like America in the mid-1900's, breaking up the one-room schoolhouses, eventually sending 90 percent of American children to government schools.

But back to my family's Irish journey...

Our vehicle carries us west along the north/south border of The Republic Of Ireland

and Great Britain, toward County Sligo, our next stop, the rare and prominent Coopershill House.

As I drive the border region, everything learned in our first four days begins to sink in, bringing on a mild, bittersweet melancholy. I am quickly becoming Irish.

But if such Celtic-fever builds, then at least it proves us headed in the right direction, west, into the Celtic heartland.

The mountains soon appear. Sligo County faces the Atlantic, just south of Donegal County. Sligo Town rules as the county seat, proclaimed the "gateway city" due to its port. Ten miles farther south we see a sign for Rivertown, the local of Coopershill House.

Coopershill welcomes us with a driveway almost one-mile long.

To the left, stand woods, and to the right, expansive fields with 10-foot high fences enclose almost 250 deer.

We drive up to the three-story, gray stone house with 17 chimneys,

and know we selected the right place.

Simon O'Hare, the proprietor, around 38 years of age, steps out to greet us.

Entering, the house boasts a center hallway, with 12-foot corridors on each floor, and a grand staircase leading from the ground floor to the second floor.

The ground floor offers a formal living room, referred to as a drawing room in English Society - thank you very much - with a warm fire crackling, mirrored by a perfect dining room capable of accommodating guests from the house's eight bedrooms.

We occupy three of the eight bedrooms, neighbored by couples from Atlanta, Belfast, Fort Worth, Geneva and Beaune.

After we sort the luggage, Simon and I immediately dive into discussion of world affairs and the debt situation, and we speculate on the look of the coming brave new world. Our worldviews share much in common. It is as if we had been discussing theses topics many times before, and were now simply catching up. We were like long lost brothers.

Noticing that the rain had stopped, I interrupt discussions and bring the family outside. My son Joe and I take advantage of the rain break to once again resume our long-toss baseball exercise. Soon the rain starts up again. But it proves a welcome relief, as deep down we all desire private time in the bedrooms before coming down at 7:00 P.M for drinks - both hard and soft.

At 7:00 PM, in the drawing room, as Simon serves drinks, we meet the other guests. The bunch of us chat up a storm, and time flies by, until Simon steps up to announce: "Dinner is served."

We find the dining room something special, with high ceilings accommodating multiple layers of oil paintings, hung, together with many objects d'art, including a Delft plate collection. The six dinner tables and three sideboards of dark mahogany underpin the Wedgwood dishes, Chrystal goblets, and Sheffield cutlery, with the sideboards holding an exquisite collection of Sterling serving platters and decanters.

Serving the soup, we enjoy our first taste; my 12-year old son saying to no one in particular: *This place is amazing*.

One thing for sure, Christina, Simon's life partner, has just demonstrated her skill as a true gourmet chef.

Over the three days we stay at Coopershill, every morsel of food proves mouth-watering, magnificent *(Christina and Simon, left)*.

Now get this. A Cooper built the house, a direct ancestor to Simon. So why is Simon's name Simon O'Hare?

I tell Simon that the Leslie estate used to comprise 24,000 acres, but that today the number stands at a mere 1,000. He, in turn, says that Coopershill also once counted 24,000 acres but today numbers 500.

So somehow the Coopers change their name and loose a lot of property. Time to dig back into history again...

Remember, in the late 1500's, Elizabeth the 1st launched the Plantation policy to tame

Ireland. It did not quite work out as planned. England did not tame Ireland, even though England established numerous 24,000-acre Plantings around much of the country.

As Elizabeth commented at the end of her life: *I find that I sent wolves, not shepherds, to govern Ireland, for they have left me nothing but ashes and carcasses to reign over!*

As a matter of fact, by the mid-1600s, the Irish became quite emboldened and staged a revolution to defy their English Norman overlords. The timing of this emboldened behavior happened, not by accident, as England itself fell into in disarray.

At the time, the Catholic Stuarts possessed the English throne, giving the Irish hope, and the Protestant English – most of the members of Parliament - did not like it.

The war in Ireland began with the rebellion of the Irish from Ulster in October 1641, resulting in the death of thousands of Scots and English Protestant settlers.

The rebellion spread throughout the country, and at Kilkenny in 1642, a political/military organization, The Confederate Catholics of Ireland, formed to conduct the Irish Catholic war effort.

This proved the perfect primordial soup to produce a take-charge kind of guy on the Protestant side, and indeed such a man presented himself: Oliver Cromwell (left).

His peers selected Cromwell to take command of the English campaign in Ireland during 1649–50. Cromwell's forces defeated the Irish Confederate/Stuart Royalist alliance, occupied the country, and destroyed the islands food supply.

The war and Cromwell's "scorched earth" tactics resulted in the massive loss of Irish life: as much as 50 percent of the Irish perished, a level of devastation comparable in the country's history only with the coming Great Hunger Famine of the 1840s.

This total defeat prevailed for the next 300 years, so Cromwell really got the job done.

Well, somehow, according to what Simone explained to me, in the mid 1800s, a man named King O'Hare, a Catholic, somehow accumulated a bit of prime land in Sligo in the neighborhood of Coopershill.

As Simon continues the story, O'Hare, a bachelor, does not want his name to die, so ... he makes a deal with the Coopers.

If they change their name to O'Hare, then he cedes his estate to them.

What's more, he promises to convert to the Church of England and pledge his loyalty to the English monarch, Queen Victoria, eventually traveling to London to do just that.

So this peculiar dynamic tells how the name change – from Cooper to O'Hare -- occurred... but how did the Leslies and O'Hares lose almost all of their land?

I will describe this shortly, but first, an excursion...

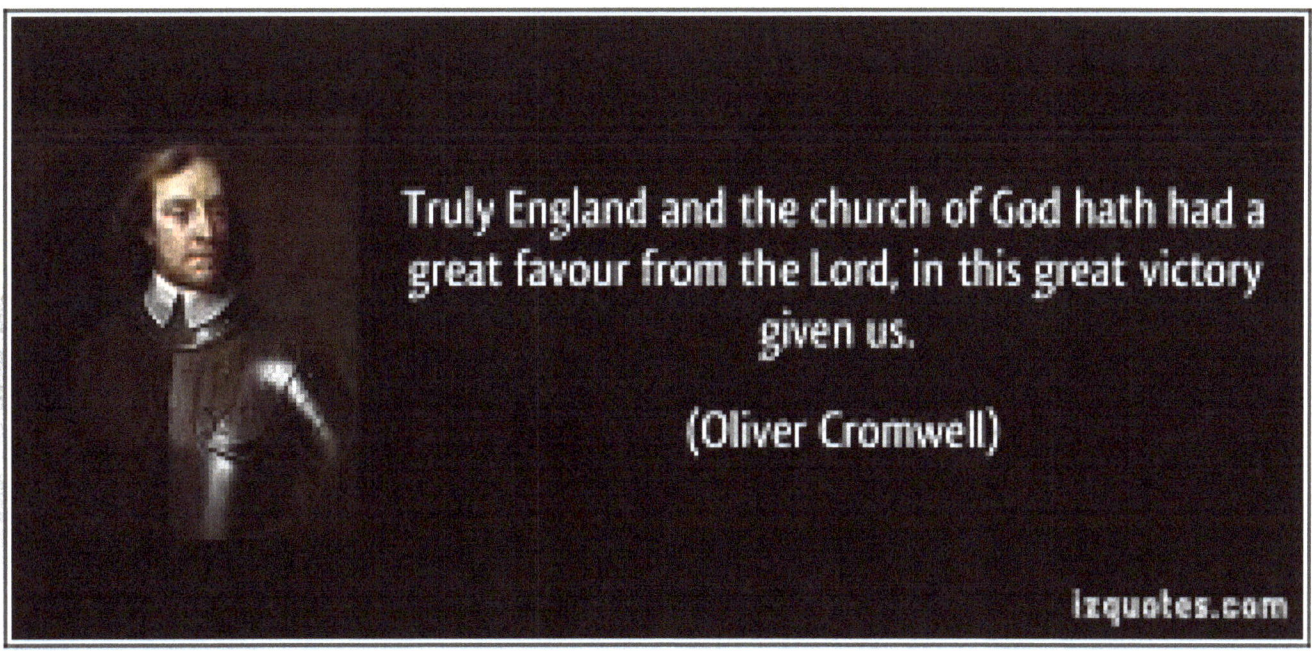

A true believer!

NOTE: Cromwell died of natural causes, but after death, his Catholic enemies (the Stuarts) regained power in England, dug his body up and hanged him (below), planting his head on a stake at the Tower of London, where it resided until the Catholics were thrown out of England for good during the "Glorious Revolution" in 1688.

DAY 6
Sunday, August 19th

Sometimes it seems that Ireland exists as pure history and nothing else, save for a bit of music.

Sure enough, on our first excursion in Sligo, history surrounds us.

In the morning we drive north for a while, almost to Donegal, to ride horses once again, but this time on open, deserted beaches.

At the stables I meet a man of my age who could prove a perfect friend to anyone given his "feet on the ground" realism, clear mind, genteel tone, and forgiving heart.

As we converse, he points out the folly of the little romantic ideas he sees in my eyes, such as my urge to purchase a piece of land in Ireland.

He gives me examples of others with big, impractical dreams. People as far away as Australia who hired him to manage properties, and to oversee construction projects.

These foreigners abandoned every one of these projects, he recounts.

Why? He asks rhetorically.

The man lived in bloody Australia for heaven's sake, running a business there, and he wants to develop a 10-acre farm on one of the islands, and, oh yes, it must be an organic farm. I told him to start with a patch of 30 feet or so and we'd see how that worked out.

And?

And he never planted a thing. I came from them islands off Donegal, and you can't know a more lonely time than that. You certainly can't be growin' things. It rains all the time, drowning everything but sheep and men.

I started to understand why the English shied away from western Ireland, leaving it to the remnants of Gaelic civilization. After more straight talk like this, my family interrupted, saying that the horses stood saddled and ready.

We mount our assigned beachcombing steeds, and head out with lead and rear guides, as my new friend wants no trouble from a bunch of romantics.

Down the lane we clip-clop in single file, and then navigate a steep path that falls to the seaside beaches.

Before taking off, I tell my new friend we had just ridden the 1,000-acre Leslie Estate, to which he replies:

When the tide is low, I have 5,000 acres of sand to ride on.

The tide *is* low, and the beach looms enormous. We begin to trot, and then the lead initiates a very long canter. We cover a lot of ground, err…, sand, finally dropping back to a walk, making our way through pools of water left behind by the retreating tide.

Then I see it!

Out on a large island, a mile away, looms a giant, fortified manor house.

I ask our young female guides for the name of this structure and the people who live in it… and the guides cannot tell me.

Its gothic architecture stands high upon the crest of the island, with vast lawns reaching all the way down to the water's edge. Behind the property sits a village.

© Suzanne Trottier

I can't take my eyes off of it. Even as we ride back, I keep turning my head for another peek.

Back at the ranch I seek out my new "perfect" friend to settle up for the ride, and ask him about the mysterious, celestial estate sitting on the edge of the Earth.

Aye, that one...

It is still privately owned. It was Lord Mountbatten's and after his passing, it was handed down to his kin. But in the 1980's there were some bombings ...

The IRA? I had to ask.

The troubles it was, and after that the family sold it to another.

Yes, that is a mountain rising in the background visible from the beach we rode upon.

As it was Sunday, my new friend recommended that I take the family to a special pub/restaurant in his village, which I did, and we enjoyed ample midday meals with gravy all around, while watching the townsfolk arrive in their Sunday finest.

As charming as lunch was, we sought to keep a schedule, mind you, as we had reserved tubs at the hot water seaweed baths for 3:00 pm, so we had to get moving.

This seaweed bath phenomenon has carried on for centuries, ever since the locals discovered that a certain species of seaweed, growing in a particular local bay, releases oil, similar to olive oil, once it sits in hot water.

Well, bring it on!

We drive out onto a peninsula jutting into the sea, a clip below Siglo Town. On this protrusion of land rises a mountain visible from every vantage point.

On the top of that mountain stands a giant Cairn looking like a boil on the mountain's high ridge. You can't take your eyes off it, and, when driving along, you remember it and again look up the mountain and find the Cairn.

It contains Queen Maeve, buried standing up 4,000 years ago, a ground floor stone-age dignitary, living with Irish rain before English torture arrived upon the scene.

The Tain March – Who Will March for Queen Maeve?

Well, you can follow marked paths up to the Cairn, but instead we soak in our seaweed baths, and save tomorrow for the queen.

DAY 7
Monday, August 20th

The entire family loved the seaweed baths. In fact, the next day my 12-year old son campaigned vigorously to take another dip.

We have nine days in Ireland, and you want to do the seaweed thing again? I mocked him.

Yes. It's better than driving all the way to Donegal!

I assured him we could do no better than to drive to Donegal, even if it meant that we wouldn't touch Queen Maeve's Cairn, and even if, as Simon advised me, it meant the whole day.

Why? My son pressed me.

Because today the entire Gaelic civilization resides in but three places: Brittany France, Western Scotland, and Western Ireland, and in Ireland, really only out in Dingle, Connemara, and Donegal. I've traveled to all of the others, so it's either today or never for Donegal.

So off we drive to the abandoned north. And now you know why we came on this trip.

We had no plan other than getting to Donegal Town for an early lunch. From the town, which sits at the civilized outskirts of Donegal County, something would present itself and our day would take form.

Donegal, as you may recall, was the third county of Ulster not included into Northern Ireland in the 1920s.

In the past, before the partitioning, Donegal had effectively possessed two centers, Donegal Town, the county seat, and Derry (AKA Londonderry). Derry went into Northern Ireland, and so today one only counts Donegal Town and its wild hills, glacially carved mountains and glens as part of Ireland proper.

By the way, though we never drove as far north as Derry (falling 30 miles short), you should know that Derry sits on the

Northwest tip of Ireland as the island's fourth largest city, and it served as headquarters for the Allied forces during the Battle of the Atlantic in WWII. At war's end, 60 German U-boats surrendered, cloistered in Derry harbor.

Arriving before noon, we find Donegal Town packed with cars... and people.

Finding a hidden car park, we buy our park-and-go ticket and proceed on foot to *The Olde Castel Pub*, an old place indeed, which I had gleaned while navigating through the center of town. After securing a table, I wander off to find the men's room, labeled "Gents" in England and Ireland.

In the passageway leading to the Gents' and Ladies' Rooms, an old map hanging on the wall catches the corner of my eye. It proves an old map of County Donegal, and it marks various locations of interest.

As of that moment, we plan to drive out another half-hour to the coast and visit the cliffs, but I hanker for something special and so it presents itself.

In very small print, the map makes mention of 250 people who abandoned their little homes in the great famine of 1846-1851.

This settlement, located in the farthest glen of Donegal, one mountain in from the western shoreline, sits in a long glen, perhaps 30 miles in length, with one road and only one little village at its starting point.

It sits in unadulterated moorland, and I feel certain that we might still find the remnants of the abandoned homesteads if we spend the day driving all the way out there and back.

Everyone knows of The Great Potato Famine. A blight starting in America spread to Europe in 1845, devastating the Irish crop in 1846. The potato had come from the Americas a century earlier, and so, too, came the blight. But the story has little to do with potatoes, and instead shows the worst sides of mankind. Let's take a look.

Ireland's 1800 population of four million people had doubled to eight million by the 1840s. At that time, the Protestant Planters reserved all the good agricultural land for grains and cattle for export to England. The little tenant farmers who worked the great estates of the landed gentry could only grow potatoes in their little plots.

In 1844, Ireland grew 10,000 tons of potatoes, with each person eating pounds of them every day. In 1846, the first year of the famine, the blight reduced the crop to 2,000 tons. Food disappeared altogether.

Remember, the system held these little tenant farmers completely boxed into their slave existence. They had no escape route to improve their lot in life, and no one obligated to step in to protect them once in dire straights.

In the 17th and 18th centuries, the penal laws prohibited Irish Catholics from owning land, from leasing land, from voting, from holding political office, from living in a corporate town or within five miles of a corporate town, from obtaining education, from entering a profession, and from doing many of other things necessary to succeed and prosper in life.

In 1846, Ireland was no longer a British colony but rather part of the national entity named The United Kingdom of Great Britain and Ireland. Unlike dominions such as Canada and Australia, The Union Act of 1801 brought Ireland directly into the fold. This is when the British designed their flag, combining those of England (which included Wales) and Scotland, with a "St. Patrick's Cross" to represent Ireland.

But why did the British, who despised the Irish, want the Irish inside the Pale? I can state my opinion on this bizarre marriage in one word: *NAPOLEON!*

Before Napoleon became dictator and then emperor of France, came the French Revolution, which followed the American Revolution.

Neither of these democratically inspired revolutions proved good for the English monarchy. France already occupied one of England's flanks, and Ireland the other. Onto the scene comes Wolfe Tone, an Irish revolutionary who sought to free Ireland by aligning with the French Catholics. In 1796, during the French Revolution, Wolfe arranges for France to send an expeditionary force of 14,000 to land in Ireland to create a beachhead there.

The contingent of French ships arrives off the coast of Ireland at Bantry Bay in December 1796, after eluding the Royal Navy. However, unremitting storms and indecisiveness combine to prevent a landing. A flabbergasted Wolfe Tone remarks: *England has had its luckiest escape since the Armada.*

This whole "surrounded by The French" image, though, proves pretty frightening in the eyes of the English, and with Napoleon suddenly on the prowl the English quickly build hundreds of Martello fortresses (above) to repel the French fleet.

These fortresses feature round stone turrets that can withstand cannon fire and deliver offensive actions against any French ship that approaches. The English position 50 or so, around Dublin and Cork. I saw one upon arriving at Dublin airport.

I bring out all of this detail to make sure that you do not think that any good will whatsoever existed between the English and the Irish leading up to the famine.

As a matter of fact the Irish have an old saying about the famine: *The Almighty, indeed, sent the potato blight, but the English created the Famine."*

In 1844 Benjamin Disraeli, England's Prime Minister, describes the problems of governing a country that has, *a starving population, an absentee aristocracy, an alien Church, and, in addition, the weakest executive in the world.*

And sure enough, two years after making these remarks, all hell breaks out in the aftermath of the potato blight.

The doubling of Ireland's population in 40 years constitutes but one of Disraeli's worries. His larger concern lies with the entire Irish economic mechanism, founded by the plantation system. And so his reference to "absentee landlords" when speaking of this debased system, explained as follows.

During the 18th century, a new approach for managing the landlord's property appeared in the form of the "middleman system", which placed the collection of rent in the hands of the landlords' agents, or middlemen.

This freed the planted plantation ones from actually being planted, and they could hang out in their fancy London apartments. The regular British realized this, and to deflect from making Irish starvation a London problem, they blamed the absentees.

This domestic political sentiment was embodied in the principal *that Irish property must support Irish poverty*.

In particular, Irish Landlords held responsibility for paying the rates of every tenant who paid less than £4 in annual rent.

They began clearing the poor tenants from their small plots, re-letting the land in larger plots for more than £4, thus reducing their debts.

Landlords evicted hundreds of thousands during the highest point of the famine, and destroyed the homes (below) to ensure the poorest tenants could not come back.

When some Irish landowners were shot by peasants, Lord Clarendon, the governor of Ireland, appealed to Parliament several times for help, but he believed that the landlords themselves held the most responsibility for the travesty in the first place, saying *It is quite true that landlords in England would not like to be shot like hares and partridges...but neither does any landlord in England turn out fifty persons at once and burn their houses over their heads, giving them no provision for the future.*

This Lord Clarendon was the one Disraeli called *the weakest executive in the world*, for being a softie.

By the time it ended, Ireland's population fell back down to four million once again.

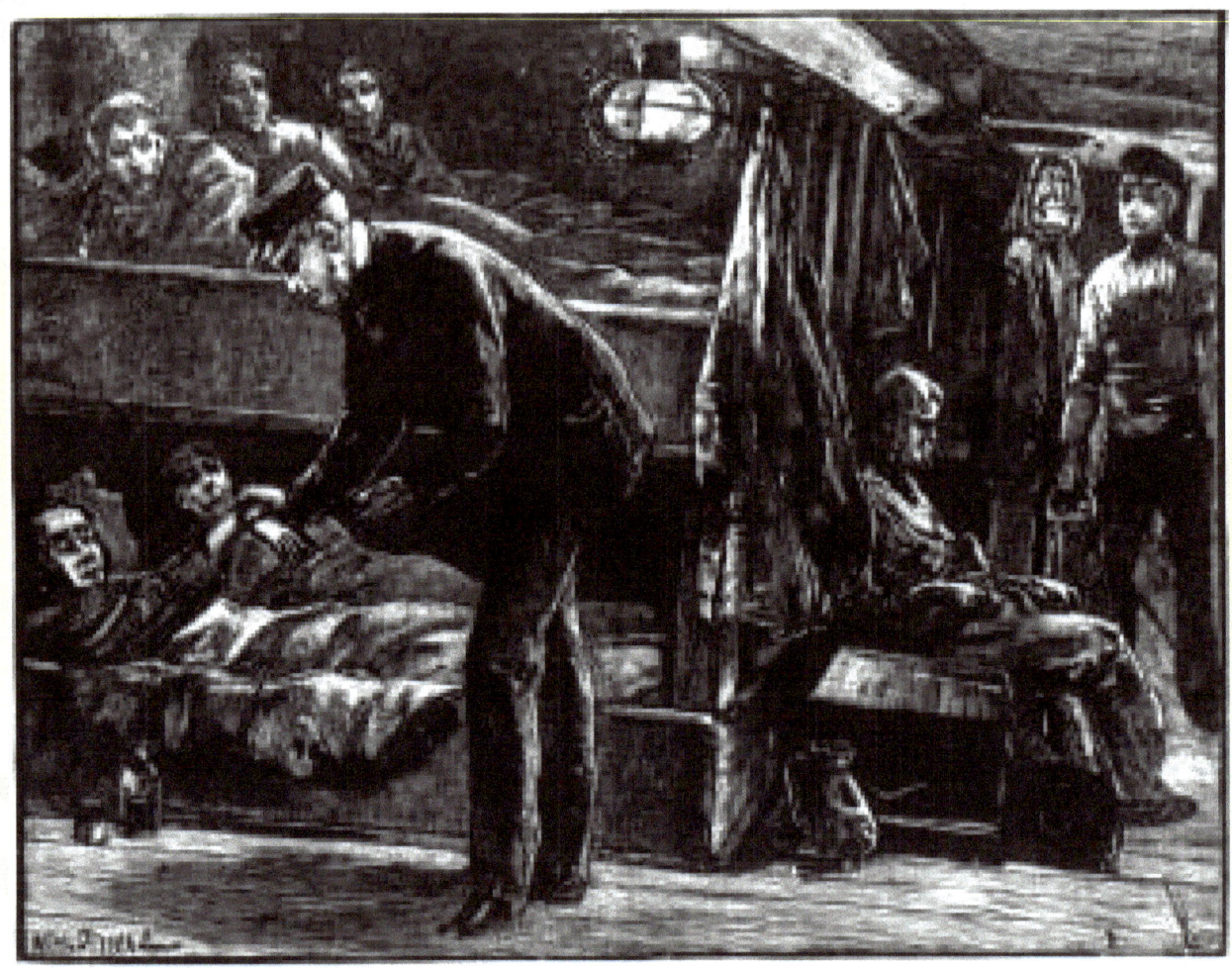

The four million lost... well, determining their exact and differing fates would prove difficult, but you get the big picture. Death by starvation and disease at home, death by starvation and disease on the "coffin ships" bringing these expatriates to America, and American citizenship for the lucky ones who made it into the slums of Boston, New York and Philadelphia ... all totaled, it added up to four million Irish souls, one-out-of-two – suddenly missing.

As one eyewitness missionary wrote: *three children huddled together, lying there because they were too weak to rise, pale and ghastly, their little limbs ... perfectly emaciated, eyes sunk, voice gone, and evidently in the last stages of actual starvation.*

So, we return to 2012, and head off for the far reaches of Donegal to find the lost settlement.

My wife Laura resumes her role of navigator. While in Donegal Town, I purchased a much-needed detailed map of the county, as getting from the town to the glen resulted in a series of roads that cut through the moorlands of the county.

As we drive, we observe the peat harvesting activities at various bogs along the way. Pausing in villages to check our map, we smell the peat burning in the fireplaces on this 60-degree day in August.

The locals built these houses, modest in size but modern in style, during the pre-2008 housing boom. The old houses remain, but no longer topped by thatched roofs.

Finally, we arrive at the village sitting at the entrance to the long glen. We pull over, and I see two old men. One simply stands across the street... just standing there. The one on my side of the road, standing at the doorway to the village pub, its peat fire burning strongly, has lost most of his teeth, but looks friendly enough, so I approach him, map in hand.

Hello. How are you doing today?

Fine, lad, I'd say the sun would be out shortly.

We're looking for the ruins.

No ruins around here that I know of.

None in the glen?

I know these parts well and can't say I know of any ruins. Might mean out in Derry.

The settlement. The one abandoned during the hunger (note, I said "hunger", not "famine").

Oh, the homes. Yes, they are still down there. After a few miles you'll get to findin' them.

I read that all 250 people left and never returned.

Most died anyway. When people leave these parts they don't come back.

I suppose not.

We had one fella that went away to Australia and made a fortune. He sent back 10 million for the hospital.

Yeah, you never know who is going to do what in the world. Well, thanks for the help.

The other guy still stood on the other side of the road when we took off.

The old glen road appears to run straight on the map, but it actually follows the stream running down the valley. We meander down the one-vehicle road.

Coming around the bend we see our first "ruin," the remains of a little two-room house that may have housed 10 people, built of stone, with a shallow fireplace where they burned the peat. Each room ran about 14 feet long and 12 feet wide.

Driving further, the houses begin popping up on both sides of the glen. We get out of our vehicle to inspect many times. The open moorland topography sits in the shadow of the big mountain beside us. The Atlantic Ocean meets the Irish shore on the other side of that mountain.

Coming down the mountain we notice a shepherd with some 20 sheep. We monitor his slow progress as we make other stops.

One settlement has two fireplaces, and it makes me wonder why they all didn't go for that, as they could certainly find enough peat.

When we find no more settlements, we reach an inland lake sitting in the moorland. It marks the beginning of a national park, and the road continues on for 30 miles all the way to Derry. I want to drive it in the worst way, but we already face the long road back to Sligo and Coopershill House.

63

DAY 8
Tuesday, August 21

Before leaving Coopershill we take a group photo of my family together with Simon, Christina, and their baby boy. The forecast calls for partly cloudy skies. Driving through the on-again, off-again rain squalls; I look forward to visiting Dublin for the first time in my life.

We drive through a fancy town with a Bank of America "Help Desk" Complex. In the 1990s, Ireland offered companies a tax-free existence if they would open up service centers in Ireland. While foregoing the tax they would not receive anyway, at least Irish employment would benefit from the resultant white-collar jobs.

It worked. Along with the rest of western civilization, Ireland prospered in the 1990's in what they termed "The Celtic Tiger." This led to expanded social programs while the money came in, then debt when it did not come in. Heavy taxation, and systemic levels of unemployment resulted – essentially the same story as what we see today in the United States and elsewhere.

I notice many newspaper articles that explain while employment levels have fallen, that academic test scores have risen.

It seems that the old grit of the Irish remains alive and well, the same grit as seen in America when the Irish clawed their way out of the slums and eventually into the White House -- think Kennedy, Reagan, and Clinton.

We soon hunger for another pub meal. As much as we loved the high-end dinners served to us at the manor houses, we nevertheless craved the pub meals just as much.

So, with 45 minutes left to go before Dublin Airport (we would drop the VW microbus off at Hertz, and take cabs into the city), we pull off the highway and make our way into a small town that boasts four pubs and two Chinese take-out storefronts.

Sitting in the pub, looking at the various patrons, some at the bar, some at the tables, I wonder where their thoughts travel... I don't mean day-to-day stuff, but nationally and politically.

Because I do not live in and for Ireland, I have difficulty visualizing the political jigsaw puzzle in comparison to how I know America. Above all, Ireland does not seem to divide itself based on strictly right- and left-policy choices, but instead always adds an element of pro- or anti-1922 treaty to the mix.

Since then there has been endless bloodshed about that issue. One famous incident, sung by U2 into stardom, was Bloody Sunday, in 1972. British soldiers right in front of the press shot two-dozen people, many of them teenagers. After that, the gloves were off, and the IRA went to town – London Town, that is - to wage a multi-decade terrorist retaliation.

On the left is 22-year old Martin McGuinness. He would play a big roll later in his life.

Gerry Adams has headed the recent incantation of Sinn Fein for decades, and Sinn Fein remains the party most bent on a unified National Ireland.

Today, Sinn Fein appears to pursue its dream through peaceful means (primarily through the efforts of Gerry Adams), but the party -- though it denies any connection to the IRA -- proves the counterparty to all of the negotiations with England in the 1970s, 1980s, and 1990s, when the IRA bombings rose to international infamy.

With unadulterated Nationalism as their central focus, the Irish also know Sinn Fein as a leftwing, socialist group.

It is the minority party.

Then we have the two splinter parties mentioned earlier:

Fianna Fail – anti-treaty, center-left, and the bastion of their leader *de Valera* until he died in 1972. Fianna Fail had retained control most of the time since 1922.

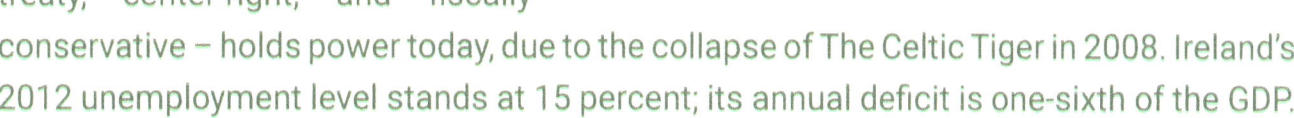

Its counterpart, Fine Gael – pro-treaty, center-right, and fiscally conservative – holds power today, due to the collapse of The Celtic Tiger in 2008. Ireland's 2012 unemployment level stands at 15 percent; its annual deficit is one-sixth of the GDP.

Another labor party exists with little regard whatsoever for the 1922 treaty, assuming its members do not lose their government jobs. Today it holds itself out as a coalition party in league with the center right Fine Gael people -- go figure.

Remember, Ireland's population totals only 4.3 million, and tens of thousands leave the country each year to find greener pastures, pun fully intended, elsewhere. Still, these political parties matter in the biggest way imaginable. Will Ireland survive in good form, or will it experience another disaster, this time of its own making?

But next up is Dublin, "Inside The Pale."

We drop off the van and our family of six and our nine bags split up into two cabs. As we enter Dublin proper, my driver starts pointing out things to me, including the tall ships moored downriver.

Crossing the river downtown, the ships offer the appearance of two hundred years hence, with the center of Dublin pretty much preserved ever since.

Passing Trinity College, we drive past the park and the Shelburne Hotel, taking a left to pull up in front of the Merion Hotel.

Now you're talking.

The kids move into a two-bedroom suite with a living room, which immediately becomes a college dorm (I only peaked inside once to see their clothes all over the place), while Laura and I occupy an inspiring room of vast dimensions, with a 20-foot high, plastered filigree ceiling, and a chandelier, a living area, and a perfect bathroom with its own entry foyer: all this at a very reasonable price, given the down economy.

Everyone heads down to the spa. Joseph and I swim, and the girls run. We agree to postpone investigation of the city until the next day. Instead, we shower and dress for dinner, meet for drinks in the public rooms next to the bar, and then move on to the Cellar Restaurant.

DAY 9
Wednesday, August 22

We hold a simple agenda. With but one day in Dublin we want the lay of the land, on both sides of the river, and we want a good lunch.

I also foster a private desire to purchase special bottles of Irish whiskey that I want to bring back stateside.

And of course, we have to visit Trinity College. (left)

First things first: we all exercise in the spa. Then we take a stroll, checking out the pedestrian streets on the south side of the river.

The kids all buy cool clothes.

We arrive at the gates of Trinity College, a major goal of the trip. You see, I attended Trinity College in Connecticut, as does my oldest daughter, and though the two Trinity schools do not officially affiliate, we do not care. We really want to visit Trinity Dublin.

I am a big fan of certain Irish writers, such as George Bernard Shaw (I have a collection of his letters), Oscar Wild, George Berkeley, Edmund Burke (a possible relative), Jonathan Swift, Bram Stoker, William Yeats, and James Joyce.

Some of them, along with others in the fields of science and mathematics, attended Trinity. All in all, Trinity College, to me, represents the intellectual hub of Ireland.

George Bernard Shaw

Inside the college gates, my eldest buys a Trinity sweatshirt. As she makes her purchase, I study a map of the campus, labeled in both English and Gaelic. I notice a street named Tara Street and its Gaelic spelling, "Teamo An Thalic." Amazingly, my daughter Tara's nickname is Teamo.

The great thing about the school, aside from academic excellence, is its location, smack in the middle of the most vibrant part of the city. If my Marshall or Burke ancestors had played their cards right, I surely would have studied here, at least for a semester.

Across the street we find the famous James Fox Cigar and Whiskey Store, established in 1881. I had looked the store up on Google before the trip and had passed it on the way in from the airport while in the cab. It remained in my cross hairs. As the Fox literature describes:

The word "whiskey" comes from the ancient Gaelic term "uisce beatha" which translates as "water of life." The world's oldest whiskey distillery still in operation is the Bushmills distillery in Ireland, which was founded in 1608. This is no surprise, as there were as many as 1200 distilleries in Ireland in the 18th century. Today, there are three distilleries in Ireland: the Cooley distillery, the Bushmills distillery, and the Middleton.

The Fox literature continues:

There are several types of Irish whiskey: Single Malt, Single Grain, Pure Pot Still and Blended Whiskey. Most of the Irish Whiskeys are distilled three times, compared to the Scotch Whiskies, which are distilled twice. Peat is not often used in the malting process, and as a result the Irish Whiskeys has a smoother finish when compared to the smoky and earthy overtones common to most Scotch Whiskies.

Well, until this trip, I never knew that they distilled Irish whiskey three times and Scotch whisky twice, and I am turning 60 next month.

What an ignoramus I've been. And I mean it; I'm supposed to know this stuff cold. Oh well, live and learn. And when you die it all goes with you. That's the Irish in me speaking, and I'm not even indulging as I write.

The rusty-haired lad at Foxes with whom I wait to speak, stands busy conversing with a woman looking to buy a traditional white-clay, long-stemmed tobacco pipe. The conversation goes on forever.

My father had such a pipe himself, which he kept up in the rafters of Keene's Steak House on West 36th Street in Manhattan, a privilege dictated to the regulars at Keene's. That pipe remains there in its nesting place, along with the thousands of others on the ceiling and walls of that wonderful Irish stronghold in NYC.

While waiting, I browse around the shop, taking in all of the exotic bottles of hooch on display. The cash register sits on a glass cabinet with a shelf below holding cigars and other interesting items.

Then I see it: an antique journal maintained by the store, opened to August of 1922, with the note: *Michael Collins funeral* scribbled in pencil.

I was in no rush after that.

Finally, my turn comes and I lay out the game plan: *a dozen of your finest Irish whiskies to bring back to The States.*

The clerk hems and haws as we look at the hundreds of bottles he must choose from.

You must have the Middleton

Ok, write it down.

And this special Jameson

Excellent, write it down.

After a while I query: How many is that?

Ten.

Then you get two more picks.

When finished, and the selection pressure waned, I ask how I can ship them to my house.

Not by post, I'm sure.

How about FedEx or DHL?

I could inquire.

Good. I'll take my family for some lunch and stop back. We'll settle up then, purchases plus shipping.

Before lunch, I notice a wax museum across the street and figure it must possess something worthwhile, something more than a J-Lo figurine.

So we stop in, and sure enough the museum offers an excellent Irish historical series. Finally, we enter a room that displays a Michael Jackson figure and the band U2. A few people stand in front of the Bono character, complaining that U2 does not pay taxes on their international revenues, and that makes Bono a #@%&.

DAY 10
Thursday, August 23, DEPARTURE

Before checking out of The Merion Hotel, I go down to the pool to increase my circulation with one last swim.

Door-to-door, our return trip will take 20 hours. Two gentlemen in their late 70s, already parting the water with their breaststrokes, clear a lane for me to join them. Soon I swim solo.

When finished, I find the same two gentlemen inside the locker room, dressing. As he buttons his trousers, one says to the other:

How's it been for you with all this rain?

The last five days have been glorious but the hundred before that, well you know ...

There's nothing to be done about it ...

We can just carry on.

We pack our bags, and each kid gets a bottle or two of the whiskey, as the James Fox people say it cannot be shipped; I am not a registered importer. Oh well!

Alan, our cabbie, drives us from The Merion to Dublin Airport. I get on well with Alan right away with all kinds of chatter. He points out that each lamppost along the way has a 3-inch splatter of yellow paint that sits on the seam of the two pipes that join to make the 10-foot post.

See them yellow marks ... there, on the posts. Every one of those posts was checked for explosives six month before the Queen came here last year.

But after they were checked couldn't someone implant the explosive?

Not without breaking the yellow seal.

Oh...

She was here for four days and appeared there (pointing to the stadium). Twenty years ago if she had done that there would have been a pair of high heels sittin' on the ground with a puff of smoke over 'em.

I laugh.

No way she could'a come here then; though she always said she wanted to.

This comment about a puff of smoke makes me recall the already-mentioned story of the bombing of Lord Mountbatten Sligo castle in the 1980's.

She wore a green dress when she arrived, the shamrock you know and she did her speech in Gaelic. Like I said, years ago she said she wanted to come to Ireland someday - if she lived long enough - and she made it. The Queen said she was sorry and she meant it. She laid flowers down. Most Irish were again' her comin' here, but by the time she left, I'd say 70 percent of the people were glad she came over.

McGuiness shook her hand

I respond: *I guess we all have to carry on, even Queens, don't we?*

Elizabeth in childhood

The next thing I knew we were in the air.

Therefore, everyman, look to that last end that is thy death and the dust that gripeth on everyman that born of woman, for as he came forth from his mother's womb so naked shall he wend him at the last for to go as he came.

James Joyce Ulysses

Joyce

RIVER LIFFEY

DUBLIN

Jerry Adams

I Meet Jerry Adams at Quinnipiac University, In Connecticut

A few weeks after returning from Ireland I was amazed to be reading an article in a local Connecticut newspaper about Jerry Adams coming to Quinnipiac University in Hamden, Connecticut. He was to inaugurate the new museum that the school had built focused both on The Great Hunger and Irish art. I felt the luck of the Irish coming my way.

I phoned my friend William Landers, who would eventually help me format this booklet. William has an Internet news site called Ameriborn News, and I wanted to see if he would cover the event. What is more, William has full reporter credentials, allowing access to people and events. Maybe we could meet Jerry.

Arriving at Quinnipiac, we lug his cameras into the gym; William presents his credentials, and we are told to set up in the isle on stage left.

We next speak to the school's PR manager, who introduces us to President John L. Lahey the school's president, who has led Quinnipiac for a few decades, elevating the school from college to university status.

We have a good talk.

I guess you could say that Mr. Lahey is all Irish, having been the grand marshal twice in New York's Saint Paddy's Day Parade and in campaigning for the funds to build the museum. Mr. Lender who he points to sitting in a chair in the front row is a major financial benefactor.

We ask about getting a post-speech interview with both President Lahey and Jerry. President Lahey says he can do it but that there is a lot of security surrounding Jerry's visit, and that the security agents will not allow Jerry to dally after the speech.

We all then get ready for Jerry to come out, with President Lahey stepping up to the podium to make the introduction.

The words Jerry spoke are in the next chapter.

The speech was interrupted a few times by pro-IRA visitors who shouted out a protest or two against the English, and against the "soft" approach Jerry and Sinn Fein were pursuing with the whole English/Irish matter. They were removed by security. After his address Jerry stayed by the podium and greeted dignitaries. President Lahey came over to William and I for his interview.

As this interview proceeded, I kept looking back and kept seeing Jerry looking over at us. I could just tell that the politician in him was kicking in. President John L Lahey was on camera and President of Sinn Fein Jerry Adams was not.

A few moments latter I heard approaching people behind me. I turned. Jerry stood smiling at me.

As William got his camera ready, Jerry and I spoke.

I told him about the book I had just penned upon my return just weeks ago from the border area of Ireland, and said that his speech, of course, was very motivating, but that it also allowed me to benchmark what I had written to what the living maker of history conveyed. I made a joke saying that my mother Mary Lou Burke (her maiden name), was worried about what I was writing, and upon hearing of my plan to attend the dedication said "listen closely to Jerry and make sure you got things right".

For the record, none of what was written in the first chapters of this book needed to be changed from what I heard from Jerry.

Myself with Jerry above

I also told him that on the trip my family went to the end of Donegal to see the abandoned village, a place he had visited many times.

William was then ready with his camera angle and he held out his microphone to start the interview.

The interview first explored Jerry's connection to his 1990's sponsor, Bill Clinton, and then dug deeper into his dramatic life leading up to that time.

In the 1960'd Jerry had come of age in a strict IRA family, with IRA members going back to the 1919 revolution. In the 1970's he was gunned down by the British (machine gunned he said), and survived multiple episodes in hospitals, and served multiple sentences in prison. And so it took to the 1980's for Jerry to decide to shun the direct confrontation methods of the IRA, and to instead pursue a political route towards peace, and eventually, towards Irish unity (Sinn Fein's ultimate goal).

Jerry got elected as a member of the British Parliament (representing his old neighborhood in Belfast), while also being elected a member of the Irish Parliament in Dublin. The long journey of using political levers, compromise, and incremental progress had begun.

Clinton, during the 1992 election campaign, decided to commit to the cause. Bill, part

Irish himself, would help Jerry, and in doing so would win over many of the 50 million Irish American voters here in the states.

After the 1992 election, Bill kept his word - to the dismay of the British government - and got George Mitchell, the former Senator from Maine, and the ex-Senate Majority Leader, to be the USA's voice inside of the UK, to champion the Irish cause with Jerry.

And over time it all worked, as can be understood by that punctuating visit to Ireland by Queen Elizabeth almost 20 years after the political channel was pioneered.

What a story.

And to think, this man, Jerry Adam, was standing in front of me, bullet hole scars and all; he was in his sixties now, but still working the room and the cause.

Above: A disposed family, painted by Daniel Macdonald, during the Great hunger episode of the 1850's.

Jerry Adams' Quinnipiac Speech

Below is Jerry Adams' Quinnipiac speech. While listening to it, Jerry's intricate Irish style required me to keep up with his stream of consciousness, the way I focus when reading Joyce's Ulysses. Jerry's sentence patterns, sudden digressions, and layers of detail have a way of transporting the listener across time to experience - almost first hand - the enormity of Ireland's legacy and its unfinished destiny.

SEPTEMBER 2012
QUINNIPIAC UNIVERSITY
HAMDEN, CONNECTICUT

Anybody here from Donegal? Anybody here from Mayo? (Waves to responders).

I want to thank Professor – President - Leahy, and this wonderful university for inviting me back again. I usually don't get invited back a second time because.... (Audience laughs). And thank you for the very, very warm welcome that you all have extended to me. And I have to say, talking to Professor Leahy and his wife, and Len, and Carla, and his son, Robert, who came down in the... we traveled together by helicopter from the Clinton Global Initiative ... that it was interesting that the driver of the helicopter was from Dublin. So, small world.

But, I was just gripping the enthusiasm and the commitment surrounding this entire museum object, and not just about telling the story about *An Ghorta Mhóir*, which is a hugely important story that needs to be told, but also as the president said, to show the Irish visual arts, to show that part of our arts is on par with anything anywhere else in the world.

So, I'm just delighted to be here, and to be playing a small role in the opening of *Músaem An Ghorta Mhóir*, Ireland's *Great Hunger Museum*. And I think it's a very invaluable new edition, very, very significant to the efforts of academics and historians, and others to tell and to understand the history of Ireland and particularly, the tragedy of *An Ghorta Mhóir*.

And *An Ghorta Mhóir*, for those of you not of the Irish tongue, is otherwise known as *The Great Hunger*. And it was one of the darkest periods in our history, and one of the most defining points in the shaping of modern Ireland, and also of causing the Diaspora – the great immigration of peoples who fled Ireland. So I commend everyone who's involved in creating this amazing and impressive project.

I think in terms of the educational and informative aspect of it, and it is all the time necessary to present the social and political context, as you can only understand history if you understand it in its time. I ... obviously, we have the benefit of hindsight and as such we have ... we can look at things much, much more clearly.

But, to understand it, we have to put ourselves in that period. And I think it's also important to reflect upon the catastrophic consequences that the sanctions taken by the government of London had for the people of the island of Ireland.

SEARCHING FOR POTATOES IN A STUBBLE FIELD.

The last time I came here, I saw the unique artworks, and I'm going to have a visit tomorrow morning, so I'm looking forward to that because they're having so much added to it. It's quite small, but very unique, but now, it has been enlarged hugely, and I look forward to seeing all of the new additions, including work by my very good friend Robert Ballagh.

But as I say to people everywhere I address, and whether it's about last week in Belfast, or 200 years ago, you cannot understand it unless you see it in the context of the English invasion, and the colonization, and more recently, in the partition of Ireland. That's the only way you can understand us as a people. If you miss that, you miss everything. And *An Ghorta Mhóir* is no different.

Leading up to the hunger in 1846, there was a dependency on the potato, there was the system of land distribution and control by English landlords, there was the growth of the population and finally, the British government's response to the potato blight. And all of these were out workings in themselves, very directly, a consequence of the out workings of colonization.

An Ghorta Mhóir was witnessed by a huge number of men and women and children fleeing to America and Canada. But the Irish have not... the famine Irish, were not ... a first wave of immigrants. Irish immigration to North America was done in the 1700s. Somewhere back then, these Catholics - fleeing the penal laws, which denied them the right to practice their religion, as well as imposing serious economic restrictions on their ability to work and to make a living – came over to America. Others were Irish Presbyterians*, who also faced discrimination because they did not belong to the English or England's established church. And some of them eventually moved on to become presidents of these United States of America and some before these, in earlier days, simply played a leadership role in the American Revolution.

---

*   My footnote: Many Irish Presbyterians in America (like Ronald Reagan) have a Scottish heritage going back to the time of James I, a Catholic English King (c 1610) who opposed Protestantism in both England and Scotland. These Scotch/Irish fled to the Belfast area in Northern Ireland, and went on to support King William III of Orange (the Protestant King, in defeating James Stuart II, (the last Catholic King) during the Battle of the Boyne in 1690. In my youth in the U.S. children from Presbyterian homes would proudly "wear the orange" on Saint Patrick's Day.

Then there was the Great Rebellion of 1917 back in Ireland, when the men and women of the Society of the United Irishmen* struck for civil rights, religious emancipation, and independence and freedom. And they lost. And they also were inspired by the American Revolution, and also by the French Revolution. Afterwards, in the 1900's, many of them fled here to the USA, others to Canada, and some to Australia.

But *An Ghorta Mhóir* raised immigration to a new level. What had been an average 5,000 Irish people leaving each year swelled to hundreds of thousands. One source has established that in the last 300 years, around 7,000,000 Irish citizens sailed to America. 7,000,000. That's greater than the population of the island at this time. It's a huge number. It's huge, given the size of our island, and it's huge as a percentage of American society. And, it's a measure of the desperate poverty that most people lived in, and of the religious and political oppression that was the norm at that time.

In the early 1840s, the population of Ireland was over 8,000,000. Over 6,000,000 of these lived in rural Ireland. Their landlords tied them with a desperate shackle to their small plots, to produce enough for their families to live on.

And most families were totally dependent on the potato. The big fields were for the landlord's business. When the blight struck in 1845, the effect was immediate. At the end of 1846, 100,000 people had crossed the Atlantic.

And today - and I was at the Clinton Global Initiative for the last few days, and we were dealing with economic and social and other difficulties across the globe, but also with the issue of famine - and we've all seen, I'm sure you've seen it, we watched it in Ireland, scenes of famine on our television screens. Most recently, in North Africa, and Somalia, and in years past in Ethiopia and you've all witnessed emaciated mothers holding tiny

---

* My Footnote: The Society of the United Irishmen was founded in 1791, and its leadership included Wolf Tone, a Protestant, and his pamphlet "Argument on Behalf of Catholics of Ireland". Tone's assertion was that the English were using religious differences to keep Ireland perpetually divided. The Society continued into the 1900's, seeking a unified Ireland.

little underweight babies with distended stomachs and glazed eyes, babies that are sometimes too weak even to cry. And you've seen the big camps where people travel for miles, perhaps as many as 60, 70, 80, 100 miles to overcrowded and often poorly resourced refugee camps. And mothers and fathers, frantically trying to save their own lives and those of their children.

Imagine that happening here. We would do that, all of us. That's what happened in Ireland. It's said that people were dead with their mouths green of the grass that they were trying to get nourishment. And those who could, left. They abandoned what were mostly one-room mud or turf walled cabins, which had sods for a roof, on these small parcels of land. And they embarked on ships, many of which would have carried African slaves, just a few decades before.

And the Irish Quarterly records that the dying lines of people in Dublin Quays ... any of you who visit Dublin, or know Dublin, down at the customs house, there's a very, very... I travel along the Quays every morning where I pass the famine memorial, Rowan Gillespie I think, was the sculptor, very, very striking stark images of skeletal figures. And the Irish Quarterly of that time, said, "A procession fraught with the most striking and most melancholic interest when in it's painful and mournful way, along the whole line of the river, to where the beautiful custom house is distinguishable in the far distance. Among the mast of the shipping, melancholy, most melancholy, is the site to the eye, not only of the Dublin citizens or resident, but to the eye of every Irish man, who is worthy to be so called and indeed the spectacle is one of sadness and foreboding. A long, continuous procession, a stream of men and women and children with their humble baggage. And these lines were often stretched for a mile and half along the river.

The famine ships left their own legacy. These coffin ships, and they were so called because of the numbers who died onboard, or who died when they reached the new world in fever camps. The journey from Ireland to Canada or to America took four weeks some cases, twice as long as that. It's estimated that 5,000 ships crisscrossed the Atlantic in those six years. They came in all shapes and sizes and the quality of their crews and the treatment of their passengers, the Jeanie Johnston, is a replica of the Jeanie Johnston is now docked at the custom house, just outside the famine memorial, and it uniquely never lost one person on board. It was run by a very, very philanthropic group of... a family, and they never lost one person.

So imagine here, you know, some of you travel back home, if you're from Ireland ... and I'll be back, God spares me, tomorrow, to watch Galway beat Mckinnon Sunday. But imagine... these ships were 60 feet long. You know, I don't know what size this room is, but 60 foot is very, very small. And you know, you would have maybe 20-foot-wide ... and visit the Jeanie Johnston if you haven't done so; it's an exact replica of the famine ship of that name, and people were fraught, people were distressed, people were stressed, people were hungry, and these small fragile vessels were to carry you below deck - in most cases - and some of the conditions were very brutal. Across this huge ocean, never to come back, never to come back, you know, you have all heard about the American Wake*, because, and it's a beautiful ...

I spend as much time as I can in Donegal, and there's a beautiful gap, there's a bridge, just a small stone bridge across the stream, the mountain stream, it's called "Droichead na Caointe,", the Bridge of Tears, because the custom was that people would have a wake for the young person who was leaving, and they'd have music and stories and so on, and then, the family walked them as far as this bridge, and that's the last you saw of them, so it's called the Bridge of Tears. And then, the children were all gone and lost ... well imagine it was your kids and you and your kids got to college or go to that somewhere else, but imagine you're never gonna see them, ever ever again.

---

* *My Footnote: An expression and song referring to the practice of a family to sit, one last time, with a departing relative about to leave on a famine boat for America.*

50 immigrant ships, 50 coffin ships sank during that period, four of them after having icebergs, and there's an interesting story, there's one ship called the Hanna, was quite remarkable because many of the crew and the passengers scrambled onboard the iceberg and the ship went down, that was in 1849 in April, and 129 of them were saved the next day by another ship which was passing.

And then there was fever, there was dysentery, there was typhus, and a man called Dr. George Douglas, who was in charge of the quarantine center on Gross Isle*

Interesting story about Gross Isle, you know, Irish America (*a magazine for U.S. citizens of Irish decent*) is very powerful, and sometimes it doesn't know just how powerful it is. But the Irish in Canada you know, they weren't as organized, they weren't as prolific in both... in commerce, the labor movement, politics, and so on and so forth, but they... there was a plan in recent times to turn Gross Isle into a national park, and it became a lightning rod for Irish Canada, or for Canadian Irish who successfully campaigned to prevent it because there were so many people from Ireland who died in the quarantine camp there. And it's 30 miles east of Quebec and this man, Dr. George Douglas, recorded his experiences.

---

*　*My Footnote: French: Grosse Île, "big island", is located in Gulf of St. Lawrence in Quebec, and is the largest burial ground of the famine outside of Ireland.*

The first ship to arrive there was called the Syria. It had 241 passengers. Nine died at sea, and one more, a little girl, a four- year old called "Ellen Keane" or "Keen", she died on arrival and was the first victim or Gross Isle. And almost 200 were admitted to the Center for typhus. Within two weeks of the establishment of the quarantine camp, he had 850 passengers in the hospital, this good doctor. There were 500 more awaiting admission onboard ships, and farther 13,000 on another 36 ships, waiting to be inspected. So just imagine that now, that, you know, of all of that 36 ships arrived with 13,000 people on them. Imagine 500 people waiting for admission into the hospital, and 850 people in the hospital. And the Virginia's a ship from Liverpool, was typical of what happened: it started with 476 passengers, 150 died on the journey, and another 106 had the fever.

And Douglas wrote, "The few that were able to come on deck were ghastly yellow, unshaven, hollow-cheeked, and without exception, the worst looking passengers I had ever seen. Not more than six or eight were really healthy, and able to exert themselves."

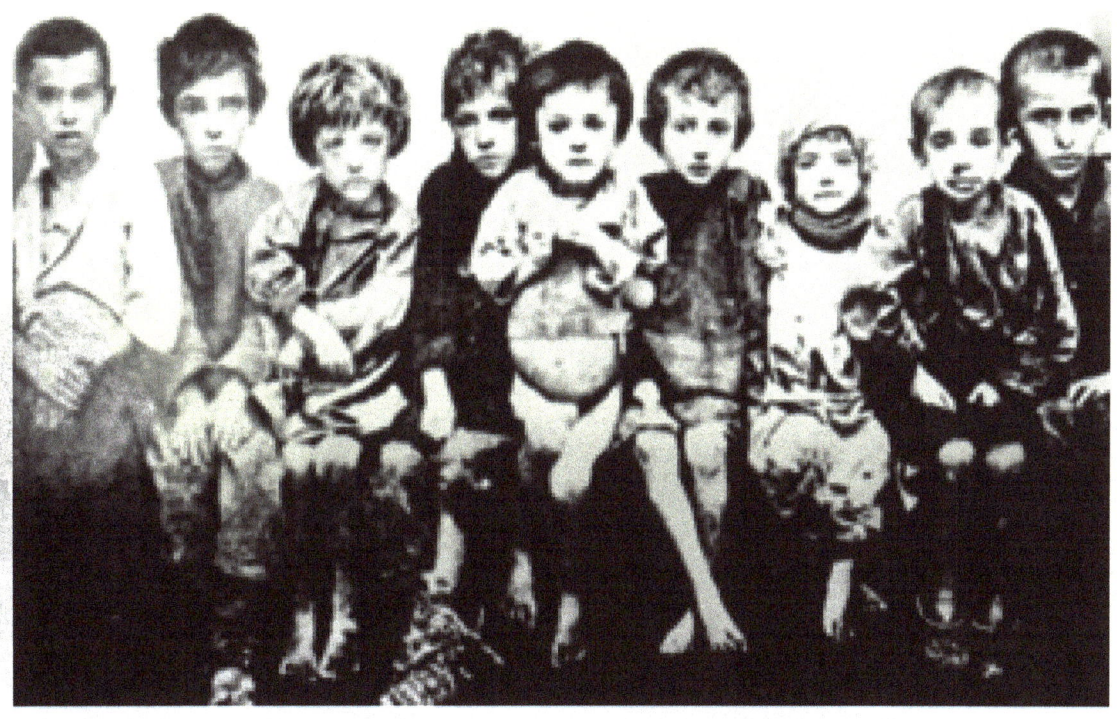

And these fever camps extended the entire east coast of the US as well as Canada. And it's important to understand, as we look back on this period, why Irish people just distinguish between the use of the word "famine" and the term "An Ghorta Mhóir," the Great Hunger. Because in a famine, there's no food. In Ireland, there was plenty of food, but not for the majority of its citizens, and the little pamphlet, I was just glancing at that the university has created, to mark the museum, actually has a list of the food that was available.

And it's a longer list than I have here, but for example, the key docks of Limerick, each day for the six years, were lined with produce for export, including pork, oats, eggs, sides of ham, and beef. And one merchant recorded the exports leaving his port from June 1846 to May 1847 - Black '47 - he's included 386,909 barrels of oats, and 46,288 barrels of wheat.

So the reality of this is appalling. And it was aptly described by George Bernard Shaw in one of his plays, Man and Superman, and one character in the play, Malone, says, "My father died of starvation in Ireland in Black '47, maybe you've heard of it?" And another character, Violet, says, "the famine?" and Malone says, "no, the starvation. When a country is full of food, and exporting it, there can be no famine."

And so, the Irish gather around the world. A few years ago, myself and Richard Macaulay, and the late Siobhan O'Hanlon visited Robben Island (off the coast of South Africa, near Cape Town), and Robben Island as you may know is where the ANC prisoners and most famously, Nelson Mandela, was imprisoned[*].

And we went there to unveil a memorial to the 10 hunger strikers who died in 1981, and the memorial is in the actual yard that Nelson Mandela used to exercise in. And, I was rather curious and I went outside the prison, just to look around, and up the wall of the prison, there was a little street sign, and it said, "Irish Town." Now, Robben Island is now a world heritage site, that's run by former prison officers, and former prisoners. So I said to one of the guys that was showing us around, "That says 'Irish Town'" and he says, "Yeah, we discovered it because the prisoners weren't allowed to go to the part of the island that they could see South Africa from, so they were usually around to the other side, and sent there to clear up this very, very heavy growth of foliage, and they discovered a graveyard. And they discovered this huge Celtic cross, and all the names were 'Murphys' and 'O'Hagans' and 'Kellys" and so forth, so they brought us down to look at this, and apparently, what happened was the ships were going through a strait, some of the passengers absconded, because the ship pulled in there, to take water onboard to get across the Indian Ocean, and this little area settlement grew up just at the very, very tip of Africa on Robben Island.

So, it's just quite amazing of where do you go when you come across Irish people. It's very amazing for us.

The greatest numbers came here. The greatest numbers came here, to the USA, even

---

[*] *My Footnote: The African National Congress (ANC) is South Africa's governing political party, since the establishment of non-racial democracy in April 1994. It defines itself as a "disciplined force of the left".*

a lot of those who went to Canada, came south into the USA, and they came here to make a new life for themselves. It was called the New Island, and, you know, it's not a way of life.

I spent a summer doing with others, Martin Furnace and other... Kathy O'Reilly and others, a tour of rural Ireland and rural communities and listening to people who were affected by the recession, and it was there that I got a real insight into the effects of immigration, 'cause then, the obvious cannot be disguised. When a football club can't field a full team, 'cause 18 of its players are in Australia, or it's young women are off and in Birmingham or Brisbane or a whole generation of GAA players just thrown to the wind, and a rural area can't be disguised.

And you know, last year, 60,000 young people left Ireland. They're tracking by this time next year, another 60,000 and it's ... the connections are quite amazing, I was up in... we were up in Leitrim (*a county in Ireland*) and this guy, who was a small builder, and obviously, the build ... the construction industry's collapsed in Ireland ... and he was running a boarding house, and so on and so forth.

But the day we were there, he was telling me he was packing a container to come back to the Bronx for work - as if he was going to the next porch - he was so familiar and you know, for someone who never really left Ireland without President Clinton giving me a visa [LAUGH], just the connectedness between the most remote part, the most rabid, wild, remote part of Ireland and different parts of the United States of America, the connection, is palpable.

And of course, the Irish have contributed hugely to the building of this United States, and they also haven't forgot their homeland, right from the very beginning. And many, you know, if you want to trace the Irish Republican content and Irish American, the Diaspora (those who immigrated to America) plead a leading role, I mean the Feeny Movement, the IRB, was founded here.*

The big event in our most recent history, in terms of national independence, in 1916, rising, a watershed event in our time, changed the very course of Irish history. The key to it was the Irish American (*the magazine*). It's said that the rising was funded by the children of the Famine. And the proclamation singles out having patiently for factor of discipline, this is proclaiming a republic, which we still haven't got yet, but proclaiming the republic having patiently for factor or discipline, of time waited for the right moment to reveal itself, she, Ireland, now seizes that moment and supported by our exiled children in America.

But relying first on her own strength, she strikes a vote of confidence, of victory. And, you know, if you're interested in following any of this up, the papers of J. J. McGarley are really ... I'm sure that they're available, see, Kristen Keneally here in the audience, I'm sure she could point you towards it ... really insightful, into that period from 1913 right through onto the 1930s, and Sean Prone has written extensively on this Irish Republican story here in the USA, and the support was crucial to what was going on at that time, and it's been crucial in more recent times.

In the 1970s, Irish America (*the magazine*) supported oppressed communities in the North (*of Ireland*), many children were brought here, many project children and other schemes, many of you opened your doors and your homes up to children from the North to provide relief from the reality of conflict and occupation, and in the 1980s, Irish America was in the front line in the efforts to end structured political and religious discrimination back home in the North with a principles campaign, and also, a legion of justice issues, from the Birmingham Six to the Guilford Four, and the internment, the use of plastic bullets, the hitch blocks and Armagh (*an Irish border county*) Prison protests, and I suppose it was really the development of the peaceful side of us, that Irish America, in our time, and the rest of the Diaspora throughout the globe, really can thank.

And the decision by Bill Clinton to become involved was down to the efforts of people here, I see Rich here in the audience as well, people like Rich and many, many more who worked hard over a long, long times, and lobbying, the Irish Americans who saw Bill

---

* *My Footnote: I do not know of the Feeny Movement or the IRB.*

Clinton before he became president, to commit to playing a more active role to achieve a full and lasting settlement of the conflict in Ireland, if he was elected. And he committed his presidency to the appointment of a special US envoy to the North, because as he said, he believed this could be a catalyst in the effort to secure a lasting peace. And they often say this, just in terms, not just of Ireland or the struggle or political campaign or activism, just in terms of life, if you want proof that one person can make a difference, here's the proof.

Because, many of us, on many issues in our own personal lives, and, you know, what we want to see in the world, will say, "I think it would be a good idea to do such and such a thing," but we never do it, you know? There are many things we don't do. But somebody had this bright idea; somebody was sitting and said to somebody else, "I think we should ask these presidential candidates would they commit to helping Ireland." Somebody had that idea, and they went and did it. And then the rest went famously. What you did was you changed US foreign policy. Someone took that point to successive governments, successive administrations not to acquiesce to the notion that this was an internal matter for the government of the United Kingdom. Butt out, it's none of your business, this is an internal matter. And that has changed.

And the '92 election the Irish Americans for Clinton became Americans for a New Irish Agenda, and they went back and pressed away for us the election promises, and in fairness, Bill Clinton did just that. The British tried to persuade him - they did so very publicly - that the media were told by a British government spokesperson in London, that its priority would be to get this notion of a special envoy scrapped. But, as I've said, Irish American for us appeared, and the president kept to what he committed to.

And in '94 I was invited by the National Committee on Foreign Policy headed up by my good friend Bill Flynn, to speak at a conference in New York. And that created a major political storm. The unions refused to attend, I remember just for those of you who are old enough, as MPs, we were barred from going to England. And I used to joke that when we're coming about, we'll have to fly around England to get here. But we also couldn't be … our voices couldn't be broadcast, on the British media. And the American media were just gob smacked by this idea. And ridiculed it so much that within a very short time, the British changed it, they got rid of the broadcasting ban, and the decision to grant the visa was a relatively small thing to do, but hugely symbolically important, the British Embassy here and the British establishment worked round the clock, against it, and claimed that it would be a diplomatic catastrophe.

And the mobilization here, I'm sure, people here around in those days, will remember. I got a 48-hour visa to visit New York, I was restricted to New York, and the backlash, back in London, was quite hysterical.

The Daily Telegraph said it was the "worst rift since Suez." I thought they were talking about something else. But Connor Cleary has written a very fine book now that this … it's really… it's a book worth… it's an inside account of the people here… of what happened. But all the other initiatives, like the appointment of Senator George Mitchell, who led a party of U.S. envoys, all of whom had a very positive role, and were significant and important players with the peace process.

So, that's what works. You know, centering, excluding, closing down, oppressing, doesn't work. Opening up, dialogue, listening, works. Works in our own lives, it works in these conflict situations.

So, on account of that came the Good Friday Agreement, and since then, because, as George Mitchell said famously to us, after we got the agreement, he said, "That's the easy bit; implementing the agreement is the hard bit."

So we've been at it ever since, we've been lead by Mark McGinness, in the North as John says, I have now shifted to Dublin, and you know, we do our best, we, about a historic mission to unite our island, so to make peace with the Unionist faction of people, to continue to mend alliances for peace and justice and for just that sense of equality, of real equality that's needed everywhere in the world, and over that period, Irish America again, has remained a constant source of support and the broad media people think it's over and everything's sorted, and so on, it isn't. It isn't sorted.

There's still work to be done, and there's still a need to keep engaged in the struggle, to keep the White House engaged, and we have a series of conferences here, in New York and San Francisco, we've got resolutions going through cities and towns across the state, and states as well, and they're all evidence of the part for potential here, and what we have to do is harness that potential. Ireland is still partitioned, the border's practically invisible, but it's still partitioned, and it's a great blight on our lives. That is the key. So we need people here to continue to be focused. We need people here to … who might be Irish or who might be have an interest in our political history, you know … to influence policy makers on Capitol Hill; it's in the US strategic interest to have Ireland united.

It's clearly in the interest of this wonderful United States of America to be supportive of that objective, so what we do need of people here is their influence with the administration, but also use their influence with the British, and with the Unionists, and the main responsibility of persuading the Unionists, obviously lies with us, who live there, but building confidence, getting rid of myths, getting rid of ignorance, tearing down fears, creating new opportunities, that's a task for everyone who wants peace and justice and freedom and Ireland.

The government have put together a constitutional convention, they have agreed reluctantly that the issue of Irish passport holders having votes in the Irish presidential elections, should be on the agenda … you know, Americans living abroad can vote for your president, the French can do the same, all sorts of society's republics can do the same, so why can't Irish passport holders have a vote in their presidential election back home? So there's lots to be done.

But I have to say, I'm very optimistic, I'm not silly, I'm not stupid, but, well, maybe I'm a wee bit stupid, but I am very optimistic about the future. And, the big, big, big lesson about ... of the period of *An Ghorta Mhóir* ... is that we're a strong people. A lesser people would have crumbled. A lesser people would have gone under. And we haven't done that and it's testimony to the durability of the human spirit. That's the case. The weight of British influence in this country, Ireland, is so great as to require a cordial union among the people of Ireland to maintain that balance which is essential to the preservation of our liberties and the extension of our commerce. Not only is it the proper thing, the moral thing, the right thing, it's also good social and economic sense that we should control our own affairs. That we would work as a people as, an island people, together to keep our people there, unless they voluntarily want to go, but no one should be forced to go.

And that's our starting point, a new union, a cordial union, between all the people of Ireland, where people can live as equal citizens in a new Ireland, and I believe that that can be achieved.

I believe that we have reconciliation, and a new partnership, so that we can have happiness and peace and prosperity and that we can have a new republic. A genuine republic, and it just makes so much sense. And we need your support for that.

So I want to thank you for the support you have given in the past, I would like to thank you if you haven't been involved, you can become involved in any way you want in the future, I want to thank the University for the great honor of being here on this unique evening, and I want to wish you all the best for the future. The very, very best and good luck to you all. Thank you very much.

Street Bowling

www.ingramcontent.com/pod-product-compliance
Lightning Source LLC
Chambersburg PA
CBHW061127070526
44584CB00033B/4248